MAJOR EMPLOYMENT-LAW PRINCIPLES

ESTABLISHED BY THE EEOC, THE OFCCP, AND THE COURTS

54
7

MAJOR EMPLOYMENT-LAW PRINCIPLES

ESTABLISHED BY THE EEOC, THE OFCCP, AND THE COURTS

(December 1964-December 1980)

Prepared by
Howard J. Anderson
Senior Editor for Labor Services
The Bureau of National Affairs, Inc.

Tennessee Tech. Library
Cookeville, Tenn.

The Bureau of National Affairs, Inc., Washington, D.C.

WITHDRAWN

316038

Copyright © 1981
The Bureau of National Affairs, Inc.
Washington, D.C.

Library of Congress Cataloging in Publication Data

Anderson, Howard J
Major employment-law principles established by the EEOC, the OFCCP, and the courts.

1. Discrimination in employment—Law and legislation—United States—Cases. I. Title.
KF3464.A7A5 344.73'01133 80-607842
ISBN 0-87179-342-3

International Standard Book Number: 0-87179-342-3

Printed in the United States of America

Preface

This volume contains a discussion of both the holdings and significance of judicial and administrative decisions in the rapidly growing field of the law of employment regulation.

The statutes involved are federal, state, and local. In the federal area, they include:

- Title VI of the Civil Rights Act of 1964—Nondiscrimination in Federally Assisted Programs (42 U.S.C. Sec. 2000d, FEP Manual 401:1)
- Title VII of the Civil Rights Act of 1964, as amended March 24, 1972, January 2, 1975, March 27, 1978, and October 31, 1978. (42 U.S.C. Sec. 2000e, FEP Manual 401:11)
- Title IX of the Civil Rights Act of 1964—Intervention by the Attorney General in Civil Rights Cases of General Importance. (42 U.S.C. Sec. 2000h-2, FEP Manual 401:41)
- Title XI of the Civil Rights Act of 1964—Jury trial, double jeopardy, authority of Attorney General. (42 U.S.C. Sec. 2000h-6, FEP Manual 401:51)
- Title I of the Civil Rights Act of 1968—Interference with Federally Protected Activities. (P.L. 90-284, FEP Manual 401:61)
- First, Fifth, Thirteenth, and Fourteenth Amendments to the U.S. Constitution. (FEP Manual 401:71)
- Civil Rights Acts of 1866, 1870, and 1871. (42 U.S.C. 1981-1983, FEP Manual 401:81)
- Executive Order 12067—Coordination of EEO Enforcement in EEOC. (FEP Manual 401:91)
- Age Discrimination in Employment Act of 1968, as amended in 1978. (P.L. 90-202, 95-256, FEP Manual 401:351)
- Equal Pay Act of 1963. (P.L. 88-38, FEP Manual 401:45)
- Vocational Rehabilitation Act of 1973. (P.L. 93-112, 95-602, FEP Manual 401:501)
- Veterans Readjustment Act of 1974. (38 U.S.C. 2012, 2014, FEP Manual 401:521)
- Executive Order 11246—Nondiscrimination under Federal Contracts. (FEP Manual 401:601)

The decisions discussed were handed down by a variety of judicial and quasi-judicial tribunals. The tribunals and their abbreviations are as follows:

- United States Supreme Court—US SupCt.
- The ten U.S. Circuit Courts of Appeals—CA, plus the number of the circuit.
- The federal district courts—USDC, plus state and district.
- The Equal Employment Opportunity Commission—EEOC.
- The Office of Federal Contract Compliance Programs—OFCCP.
- State Courts—designation of the state and court by initials.

A detailed table of contents and a table of cases are included to assist the user in finding the cases discussed. References used throughout the text and in the table of cases are to decisions as published in BNA's *Labor Relations Reporter*. For decisions, the citations are to volume and page in the LRR volumes of (1) Fair Employment Practice cases (e.g., 16 FEP Cases 146), (2) Labor Relations Reference Manual (e.g., 66 LRRM 1269), or (3) Wage and Hour Cases (e.g., 10 WH Cases 488). For statutes, the citations are to pages in Fair Employment Practices Manual (e.g., FEP Manual 401:101).

Table of Contents

Civil Rights Act of 1871

Equal Pay Act of 1963

Age Discrimination in Employment Act

Issue	Holding	Comment
Bona Fide Benefit Plan: Compulsory Retirement	The involuntary retirement of a 60-year old employee under the terms of a retirement plan established in 1941 did not violate the Age Discrimination in Employment Act (ADEA), as originally enacted in 1967. Section 4(b)(2) of the original Act provides that it shall not be unlawful for an employer "to observe the terms of a bona fide seniority system or any bona fide employee benefit plan, such as a retirement, pension, or insurance plan which is not a subterfuge to evade the purposes of the Act." In holding that the retirement did not violate the Act, the majority opinion by Chief Justice Burger stated that the retirement had occurred pursuant to a bona fide employee benefit plan under Sec. 4(f)(2). There is nothing to indicate, the opinion added, that Congress intended wholesale invalidation of retirement plans adopted in good faith before the passage of the Act or to require employers to show business or economic purpose to justify such plans. Justices Stewart and White wrote concurring opinions. Justice Marshall was joined by Justice Brennan in dissenting. (United Air Lines, Inc. v. McMann, US SupCt-1977, 16 FEP Cases 146)	In the 1978 amendments to ADEA, Congress added language to Sec. 4(f)(2) designed specifically to overrule McMann v. United Air Lines. As amended, Section 4(f)(2) provides that: "No such seniority system or employee benefit plan shall require or permit the involuntary retirement of any individual specified by Section 12(a) of this Act because of the age of such individual." The legislative history makes it clear that the intent of this amendment was to overrule the McMann decision and prohibit employers from applying pre-ADEA retirement plans to require the retirement of employees prior to age 70. Enacted in 1967, ADEA seeks to promote the employment of older persons based on their ability instead of their age. It prohibits discrimination in employment against persons between the ages of 40 and 70. The original Act set the ages between 40 and 65, but in 1978 Congress amended the Act to raise the top age to 70. The prohibitions apply when at least one of the employees involved in the alleged discrimination is in the 40 to 70 age bracket. But there also may be unlawful discrimination if both employees are within the age bracket. If, for example, a 50-year-old employee claims he is being discriminated against in favor of a 45-year-old employee, there could still be a violation.
Bona Fide Benefit Plan: Federal Employers—Foreign Service	It is constitutional to require employees of the U.S. Government who are covered by the Foreign Service retirement and disability system to retire at age 60. In finding that the age-60 retirement rule does not violate the Equal Protection Clause of the Fifth Amendment to the Constitution, the Supreme Court said that the compulsory retirement of Foreign Service officers at age 60 furthers the goal of assuring their professional competence. The decision was by an eight-to-one margin, with Justice Marshall the lone dissenter. (Vance v. Bradley, US	At the time the action was brought, employees covered by the Civil Service retirement system were not required to retire until age 70. Under the 1978 amendments to the Age Discrimination in Employment Act (ADEA), federal employees are not subject to any mandatory retirement age. In upholding the age-60 mandatory retirement for Foreign Service officers, the Court said that opponents of the mandatory retirement age failed to demonstrate that Congress had no reasonable basis for believing that conditions overseas generally are more

Issue	Holding	Comment
Bona Fide Benefit Plan: Compulsory Retirement—Contd.	SupCt-1979, 19 FEP Cases 1)	demanding than conditions in the U.S., and that at age 60 or before many persons begin to decline in mental and physical reliability.
Bona Fide Benefit Plan: State Employees	In two cases involving state employees, the Supreme Court upheld a Massachusetts statute requiring retirement of state police officers at age 50, and a Louisiana statute compelling retirement at age 65 of nonelected, nonappointed state employees eligible to retire under either the Social Security Act or any public employee retirement system. The Court found that neither statute violated the Equal Protection Clause of the Fourteenth Amendment to the Constitution. (Mass. Board of Retirement v. Murgia, US SupCt-1979, 12 FEP Cases 1569; Cannon v. Gusti, US SupCt-1975, 11 FEP Cases 715)	Since both of these cases were filed under the Equal Protection Clause of the Constitution, there was no ruling on the effect of Title VII on the mandatory retirement aspect of the cases or the effect of the congressional action providing that no seniority system exempt under Section4(b)(2) of the Age Act shall require or permit the involuntary retirement of any individual specified by Section 12(a) of the Act because of the age of such individual.
Bona Fide Occupational Qualification (BFOQ)	As under Title VII of the Civil Rights Act that forbids employment discrimination based on race, color, religion, sex or national origin, the Age Discrimination Act includes an exemption permitting an employer to differentiate as to age if it is shown to be a "bona fide occupational qualification reasonably necessary to the normal operation of the particular business." In a leading case on this exemption, the U.S. Court of Appeals for the Seventh Circuit held that Greyhound Bus Lines had to demonstrate a rational basis in fact to believe that the elimination of its maximum age of 40 for hiring would increase the likelihood of harm to its passengers. But the court added that evidence of only a minimal increase of risk of harm was enough to justify Greyhound's policy. (Hodgson v. Greyhound Lines, Inc., CA 7-1974, 7 FEP Cases 817, cert. denied by US SupCt-1975, 9 FEP Cases 58)	In arguing for judicial support of its rule, Greyhound stressed that its business was the safe transportation of its passengers.
	In a case in which a petition for a hearing was denied, the Fifth Circuit contrasted the difference between a defense based on a bona fide occupational qualification and one based on good cause or reasonable factors other than age. The court said that a BFOQ is an affirmative defense, and the burden of persuasion is borne by the employer. But a defense of good cause or differentiating factors other than age does not bear with it the burden of ultimate proof. The defendant's burden is only that of going for-	

Issue	Holding	Comment
Bona Fide Occupational Qualification (BFOQ)—Contd.	ward with the evidence. The plaintiff retains the burden of proving by a preponderance of the evidence that age was a determining factor. (Marshall v. Westinghouse Electric Corp., CA 5-1978, 17 FEP Cases 1288, 18 FEP Cases 501)	
	In a later case, the Fifth Circuit upheld a bus line's policy of not hiring anyone over age 40 as an intercity bus driver. It said that a public carrier might continually strive to employ the most qualified persons, since the essence of the business is the safe transportation of passengers. (Usery v. Tamiami Trail Tours, CA 5-1976, 12 FEP Cases 1233) But see Houghton v. McDonnell Douglas Corp., CA 8-1977, 14 FEP Cases 1594, in which a bona fide occupational qualification defense for the termination of a 52-year old test pilot was rejected. The court said the employer did not meet its burden of proving that "substantially all of the older pilots are unable to perform the duties of test pilot safely and efficiently or that some older pilots possess traits precluding safe and efficient job performance unascertainable other than through knowledge of the pilot's age."	As in the Greyhound case, the bus company stressed that its business was the safe transportation of passengers. Other examples of possible BFOQ exceptions are: ● Federal statutory and regulatory requirements that impose a compulsory age limitation, such as the Federal Aviation Agency regulation setting a ceiling of age 60 for pilots. ● Actors required for youthful or elderly roles. ● Persons used to advertise or promote the sale of products for youthful or elderly customers.
Conciliation Requirement	Under Section 7(b)(2) of the Act, there is a mandate that the Labor Department's compliance officer "promptly seek to eliminate any alleged unlawful practice by informal methods of conciliation, conference, and persuasion." The U.S. Court of Appeals for the Eighth Circuit upheld a lower court decision refusing to stay proceedings to permit the Labor Department time to make necessary efforts to effectuate voluntary compliance. This was a matter within the discretion of the district court, the appeals court said. (Brennan v. Ace Hardware Corp., CA 8-1974, 7 FEP Cases 657)	Title VII of the Civil Rights Act of 1964 contains a similar provision requiring the EEOC to seek to eliminate unlawful practices by the informal methods of conference, conciliation, and persuasion. Prior to the 1972 amendments, which gave the EEOC the right to bring an action in court, the courts were liberal in construing the procedural requirements. Since the amendments, they have been more strict. See below under "Civil Rights Act, Title VII: Procedures" for discussion of cases involving procedures under Title VII.
	Because the Secretary of Labor made a sufficient attempt at conciliating an age discrimination complaint under ADEA to meet the minimum jurisdictional requirement, a federal district court should not have dismissed the Secretary's action. So ruling, the Tenth Circuit ordered the lower court to stay the action pending further attempts at conciliation. Enforcement of the ADEA, the appeals court observed, would be hampered severely if courts	In its opinion, the appeals court acknowledged that the Secretary had not complied with the statutory directive that enforcement of the ADEA be effected wherever possible. With more than a month to go before the statute of limitations was to run, the Secretary conditioned further negotiations on the employer's agreement to waive the limitations period. The employer refused to do so, and negotiations broke off. The court said the employer was

Issue	Holding	Comment
Conciliation Requirement—Contd.	were to demand full compliance with a standard that conciliation be "exhaustively" attempted upon pain of dismissal of the complaint. The court pointed out that Labor Department officials made a substantial initial effort to effect compliance; that they informed the employer of the specific allegations of misconduct; and that they told the employer what action was necessary to comply with the Act. Once there has been a significant effort to effect voluntary compliance, if the district court finds that further conciliation efforts are required, "the proper course is to stay proceedings until such informal conciliation can be concluded." (Marshall v. Sun Oil Co. of Pa., CA 10-1979, 18 FEP Cases 1632)	under no obligation to waive the statute of limitations and the Secretary's insistence that it do so "prematurely restricted the conciliation process." Administration and enforcement of the ADEA were originally entrusted to the Department of Labor. But a reorganization plan in 1978 transferred these functions to the EEOC effective July 1, 1979.
	Whether the court determines that the Secretary of Labor (now EEOC) engaged in sufficient conciliation efforts to permit action against an employer to go forward under the Age Discrimination in Employment Act will depend in large part on the conduct of the employer. The adequacy of the conciliation efforts depends on three things: what the agency did originally, how the employer responded, and how the Secretary reacted to the employer's action or inaction. A lower court judgment dismissing an action by the Secretary was remanded. (Marshall v. Sun Oil Co., CA 5-1979, 21 FEP Cases 257)	The court held that the government is not required during conciliation to prove each specific instance of discrimination with great particularity; nor is it required to present as much evidence as would be needed to prevail at trial. This would reward the large scale discriminator and undermine the legislative goal of obtaining voluntary compliance in such cases. In this case, the Secretary presented the employer with evidence establishing a prima facie case of age discrimination, but the employer refused to discuss or rebut the evidence. The Secretary had no obligation to investigate further.
Constitutionality	The application of the Age Discrimination in Employment Act to a school board does not violate the Commerce Clause of the U.S. Constitution, notwithstanding the U.S. Supreme Court's decision in National League of Cities v. Usery, US SupCt-1976, 22 WH Cases 1064, that the Commerce Clause does not permit Congress to apply the wage and overtime provisions of the Fair Labor Standards Act to integral operations of state and local governments. The reasons are: (1) the school board's policy choice to discriminate on the basis of age in selecting individuals for employment is outweighed by the significant national interest in ensuring nondiscriminatory employment practices in areas affecting interstate commerce, even assuming that public education represents an integral state government operation; and (2) the degree of federal intrusion into this area of state	In a later decision, the court found specific violations of the Act in the school board's failure to give consideration to a junior high school counselor's application for an administrative position. The court found that the action was based on the fact that the counselor had only one year remaining before he would be required to retire under a mandatory retirement law. (Marshall v. Board of Education of Salt Lake City, USDC Utah–1977, 15 FEP Cases 368) Another court upheld the extension of the ADEA to states and their political subdivisions, finding that it was a constitutional exercise of the power of Congress under the Commerce Clause of the Constitution and Section 5 of the Fourteenth Amendment. (EEOC v. Florissant Valley Fire District, USDC EMo–1979, 21 FEP Cases 973)

Issue	Holding	Comment
Constitutionality—Contd.	concern is minimal in that ADEA imposes only the limited negative obligation not to use age arbitrarily as an employment criterion, rather than an affirmative obligation to restructure the school board's integral operation. (Usery v. Board of Education of Salt Lake City, USDC Utah-1976, 13 FEP Cases 717)	
Damages: Recovery	Compensatory damages for physical pain and suffering may not be recovered under ADEA. (1) "Legal damages" under the ADEA were limited to back pay and "liquidated damages," because the statute specifically mentioned recoverable money damages only in reference to the term "amounts," (2) Congress concluded that "the resumption of productive work removes the root of emotional anxiety" resulting from age-based discrimination, making compensatory damages unnecessary; (3) because compensatory damages will be abused by plaintiffs and be subject to misunderstanding by a jury, damages would not be limited to compensation for actual injury, but would be primarily punitive in nature; and (4) allowance of compensatory damages might undercut the role of the conciliation process in the statutory scheme, because claimants would be less willing to accept an out-of-court settlement where they could hope for a large verdict for pain and suffering. (Rogers v. Exxon Research and Engineering Co., CA 3-1977, 14 FEP Cases 518)	The decision by the Third Circuit reversed a district court holding that an employee who claimed he was discharged because of his age could seek damages under ADEA for physical and mental suffering. (USDC NJ-1975, 11 FEP Cases 1447) In a case decided after the 1978 amendments to ADEA, a court held that punitive damages and damages for emotional distress or mental illness are not available under ADEA. The Conference Report on the amendments, the court said, demonstrates that the provision for "legal relief" refers only to unpaid minimum wages or overtime compensation and liquidated damages categories under Section 7(b) of ADEA. (Riddle v. Getty Refining & Marketing Co., USDC NOkla-1978, 18 FEP Cases 1072)
Employee Evaluation as Basis for Action	The ADEA does not require use of formal evaluation procedures to establish as a matter of law that discharges were for reasons other than age. So ruling, the Eighth Circuit upheld a district court finding that a company did not violate ADEA by discharging four employees over age 53 after acquiring a financially troubled company and reorganizing the sales department. Evidence to rebut a prima facie case of discrimination came from a subjective explanation by a newly appointed general sales manager who testified that one employee was a supervisor for servicing a customer who had made various complaints; that another employee had had prior difficulties in warehouse work and had no major supervisory responsibility; that the third employee lacked any clear responsibilities at the time of the reorganization; and that the fourth employee had been blinded in	Prior to the Cova decision, some district courts had upheld evaluations of employee ability and job performance as reasonable factors, other than age, in upholding terminations of older workers. (See Stringfellow v. Monsanto Co., USDC WArk-1970, 3 FEP Cases 22; Gill v. Union Carbide Corp., USDC ETenn-1973, 7 FEP Cases 571)

Issue	Holding	Comment
Employee Evaluation as Basis for Action—Contd.	one eye, which the sales manager believed affected his work ability. (Cova v. Coca Cola Bottling Co., CA 8-1978, 17 FEP Cases 448)	
Help-Wanted Ads	The Labor Department has taken the position that no indication of a preference based on age may be included in help-wanted ads. This would bar such terms as "age 25-35," "under 40," or descriptive words such as "young," "boy," or "girl." These interpretations have been litigated with mixed results. Some examples of holdings are:	The Labor Department has also issued interpretations concerning the use of tests in hiring and promotion. Because of the increasing use of tests, it takes the position that younger workers tend to be more "test-sophisticated" than older workers. For this reason, the Department scrutinizes the selection procedure closely when tests are the only determining factor.
	● An employment agency violated ADEA by placing "help-wanted" advertisements in newpapers indicating preference for a "girl." The court stated that the Labor Department's interpretation was entitled to "great deference" and that the ads indicated a prejudice against individuals over 40. (Hodgson v. Career Counsellors International, Inc., NSDC NI11-1972, 5 FEP Cases 129)	See below under "Civil Rights Acts, Title VII: Substantive Rulings—Sex Discrimination, Newspaper Advertising" for rulings under Title VII on discrimination in help-wanted ads.
	● An employment agency did not engage in illegal age discrimination by placing help-wanted ads for "college students," "girls," "boys," and "June graduates." The court said that ADEA does not forbid employers from encouraging young persons from turning from idleness to useful endeavor. (Brennan v. Paragon Employment Agency, USDC SNY-1973, 5 FEP Cases 915, affirmed by CA 2-1974, 7 FEP Cases 1258)	
	● Help-wanted advertisements directed to "recent graduates" did not automatically violate ADEA. If the ads are part of a general invitation to a specific class of prospective customers coming into the job market at a particular time of the year, there is no violation. But if the phrase is used in reference to a specific job opportunity, there would be a violation of the Act as implying older persons need not apply. The effect is determined by the context, not the words. (Hodgson v. Approved Personnel Service, CA 4-1975, 11 FEP Cases 688)	
Procedures: Burden of Proof—Prima Facie Case	Both the formula for establishing a prima facie case and the order of proof that the U.S. Supreme Court adopted in McDonnell Douglas	In the court's view, the McDonnell Douglas formula appropriately adapted, can meet the problem of proof in any discrimination case in

Issue	Holding	Comment
Procedures: Burden of Proof—Prima Facie Case—Contd.	Corp. v. Green, US SupCt-1973, 5 FEP Cases 965, for actions under Title VII apply, with some modification, to an action under the Age Discrimination in Employment Act (ADEA) that is tried by a jury. But the trial judge should not read the formula to the jury. Under the McDonnell Douglas formula, the complainant has the burden of establishing a prima facie case. If he does so, the employer must then state a valid reason for the complainant's rejection or discharge. The complainant then has an opportunity to prove this reason is pretextual. Proof of a prima facie case may be accomplished by establishing that the complainant is a member of a protected class, that he was qualified for the job, that he was rejected or replaced, and that the employer sought someone else to fill the job. (Loeb v. Textron, Inc., CA 1-1979, 20 FEP Cases 29).	which motivation is an issue. In an age case, it added, the complainant does not have to prove he was replaced by a younger person or a person outside the protected age group. A dischargee need show only that he was doing his job well enough to rule out the possibility that his discharge was for inadequate performance and that the employer sought a replacement with qualifications similar to his own. (See also Laugesen v. Anaconda Co., CA 6-1975, 10 FEP Cases 567)
Procedures: Burden of Proof—Rebutting Prima Facie Case	A company that discharged an employee for incompetence is not required by ADEA to prove that it applied the same standards to all other similarly situated employees in order to rebut a prima facie case of age discrimination. The employee was discharged, the company alleged, for failure to maintain proper communication with general contractor personnel, submitting progress billings late or incompletely, failing to communicate with his immediate superior, and failing to service customer complaints properly. The Labor Department argued that because the employer's defense was that the discharge was for good cause, the burden should be on the employer to demonstrate that the differentiating factors other than age that resulted in the employee's discharge were criteria that were applied to all other workers who were similarly situated. The court noted that the ADEA provides three defenses for an employer accused of discharging an employee because of age. They are: (1) Age is a bona fide occupational qualification. (2) The discharge was based on factors other than age. (3) The discharge was for good cause. Bona fide occupational qualification, the court stated, has been treated as an affirmative defense, requiring the employer to carry the burden of persuasion. In contrast, the court added, the exceptions of good cause and differentiating factors other than age have not been treated as shifting the burden of persuasion to the employer. Instead,	The court took note of its earlier decision that an employer is required to prove by a preponderance of the evidence some legitimate, nondiscriminatory reason for a discharge that is alleged to constitute racial discrimination. (Turner v. Texas Instruments, Inc., CA 5-1977, 15 FEP Cases 746) It also said that the extent to which cases arising under Title VII of the Civil Rights Act of 1964 govern cases under ADEA is not clear. But it added that some distinction between the two types of cases is possible. If the employer were required to prove that its criteria of differentiating factors were applied to all similarly situated employees, this would require the employer to prove that its asserted cause was "non-pretextual." Such a requirement, the court concluded, is inconsistent with both its prior ADEA decisions and case law under Title VII. The Fifth Circuit later denied a rehearing in the Marshall case. (Marshall v. Westinghouse Electric Corp., CA 5-1978, 18 FEP Cases 501)

Issue	Holding	Comment
Procedures: Burden of Proof—Rebutting Prima Facie Case—Contd.	the employer is required only to "go forward" with evidence demonstrating factors other than age as a basis for the discharge. (Marshall v. Westinghouse Electric Corp., CA 5-1978, 17 FEP Cases 1288)	
Procedures: Jury Trial—Government Action	Because the right to trial by jury is one of the most precious rights guaranteed by the U.S. Constitution, the Secretary of Labor (now the EEOC) should be granted a jury trial in an action under ADEA, according to a federal district court in Iowa. The court noted that ADEA does not explicitly forbid jury trials for actions brought by the Government. Since ADEA provides for a jury trial in actions to recover amounts owing, regardless of whether equitable relief is sought, the court stated, there is no reason to deny a jury trial on issues of fact merely because reinstatement or other equitable relief is sought in addition to legal remedies, such as back wages and monetary damages. (EEOC v. Blue Star Foods, Inc., USDC Iowa-1980, 22 FEP Cases 504)	The court observed that no other case had discussed this question. If there is no right to a jury trial in actions brought by the Government, it added, an individual's right to a jury trial could be circumvented merely by the commencement of an action by the Government.
Procedures: Jury Trial—Private Action	A jury trial is available where sought by one of the parties in an action under ADEA for lost wages, even though ADEA, as originally enacted, contained no provision expressly granting a right to a jury trial. Congress intended that ADEA be enforced in accordance with the procedures of the Fair Labor Standards Act, under which there is a right to a jury trial, rather than pursuant to Title VII of the Civil Rights Act of 1964, under which the award of back pay is a matter of equitable discretion. Section 7(b) of ADEA empowers a federal district court to grant "legal" as well as equitable relief, and the Seventh Amendment to the U.S. Constitution provides a right to a jury trial in cases in which legal relief may be granted. The decision was unanimous, with Justice Blackmun not participating. (Lorillard v. Pons, US SupCt-1978, 16 FEP Cases 885)	Although the right to a jury trial had been upheld in actions brought by employees under the Fair Labor Standards Act, no right to a jury trial had been recognized by the courts in actions brought by the Secretary of Labor to enjoin violations and compel payment of unlawfully withheld minimum wages or overtime compensation. (See Sullivan v. Wirtz, CA 5-1966, 17 WH Cases 284) An amendment to ADEA adopted in 1978 specifically provides that "a person shall be entitled to a trial by jury of any issue of fact in any such action for amounts owing as a result of a violation of this Act, regardless of whether equitable relief is sought by any party in such action."
Procedures: Notice of Intent to Sue	Under Section 7(d) of ADEA, an aggrieved individual must give the Secretary of Labor not less than 60 days' notice of an intent to file an action. Moreover, the notice of intent to sue must be filed within 180 days after the alleged unlawful practice occurred. But the Fifth Cir-	Where the alleged violation takes place in a state that has an age discrimination law, the notice of intent to sue must be filed within 300 days after the alleged unlawful practice occurred or within 30 days after the receipt of notice of the termination of proceedings under

Issue	Holding	Comment
Procedures: Notice of Intent to Sue—Contd.	cuit held that the 180-day period may be tolled where the employee did not have an opportunity to learn of his rights under the Act. (Charlier v. S.C. Johnson & Son, Inc., CA 5-1977, 15 FEP Cases 421)	the state law, whichever is earlier. When the Secretary receives notice of intent to sue, he is required to seek to eliminate any unlawful practice by the informal methods of conciliation, conference, and persuasion. The filing of a suit by the Secretary terminates the individual's right to sue.
	The requirement of Section 7(d) of ADEA that a notice of intent to sue be filed with the Secretary of Labor within 180 days after the alleged discriminatory act as a precondition to a private action under the Act may not be waived, but the requirement is subject to possible tolling and estoppel. The following circumstances warranted the tolling of the 180-day period: (1) The employee consulted an attorney who told her to take her complaint to the local Wage-Hour Division office, which she did promptly. (2) The assistant area director told her that it might take up to a year before an investigation was concluded. (3) She telephoned him at least once a month, but she was not told until the 180-day period had run that she was required to file a notice of intent to sue. (4) Upon learning this, she immediately retained another attorney who promptly filed the notice 36 days beyond the statutory time period. (5) The employer was contacted by the Labor Department on the same day she registered her allegations of age discrimination, and the Department attempted to conciliate her complaint well before receiving her notice of intent to sue. (6) The assistant area director customarily advised every complainant of the 180-day notice requirement, but he did not do so in this instance. (7) His delay in advising the former employee of the notice requirement was due in fact to his decision that, before doing so, he would await certain statistical information that the employer had agreed to supply. (Dartt v. Shell Oil Co., CA 10-1976, 13 FEP Cases 12) This was affirmed by an equally divided Supreme Court. (Shell Oil Co. v. Dartt, US SupCt-1977, 16 FEP Cases 146)	
	A plaintiff's letter to the Labor Department stating that it was her wish that the Department bring an action under the Act did not meet the notice requirement of section 7(d) of ADEA. The notice requirement is jurisdictional in nature and so must be strictly applied. More-	The 180-day notice requirement was also found to be jurisdictional in Oshira v. Pan American World Airways, USDC Hawaii-1974, 8 FEP Cases 446. The plaintiff was not permitted to add five additional plaintiffs who had not filed notices with the Secretary of

Issue	Holding	Comment
Procedures: Notice of Intent to Sue—Contd.	over, the employer's refusal to hire the applicant was not a continuing violation so as to postpone the running of the 180-day notice period. (Powell v. Southwestern Bell Telephone Co., CA 5-1974, 8 FEP Cases 1)	Labor. An employer's failure to post the required Section 8 notice explaining the purposes of the Act was held by another court not to excuse the plaintiff's failure to file the 180-day notice. (Hiscott v. General Electric Co., USDC NOhio-1974, 8 FEP Cases 1003) But this case should be compared with Bishop v. Jelleff Associates, USDC DC-1974, 7 FEP Cases 510.
	A discharged employee's oral complaint that he had suffered age discrimination is not sufficient to constitute notice of filing intent to sue that is a prerequisite to a suit under ADEA. (Carter v. Crown Hosiery Mills, Inc., CA 4-1980, 22 FEP Cases 1818, affirming USDC MNC-1978, 22 FEP Cases I816)	The decision originally was unpublished. The Fourth Circuit's holding later was denied review by the U.S. Supreme Court. (Carter v. Crown Hosiery Mills, Inc., US SupCt-1980, 22 FEP Cases 1832)
	An employee's termination date, for the purpose of determining whether his notice of intent to sue was timely filed with the Secretary of Labor, is the date on which he received unequivocal notice of termination and ceased to render further services to the employer. It is not the subsequent date on which he received his last paycheck and on which the company benefits terminated, even though another circuit ruled in Moses v. Falstaff Brewing Corp., CA 8-1975, 11 FEP Cases 828, that the official termination date as reflected in company records should be considered the date of termination. A company may use different termination dates for different purposes, and determination of timeliness of an employee's lawsuit against the employer based solely on records that are within the employer's exclusive control would be looked upon with disfavor, as would a rule penalizing an employer for giving an employee extended benefits after the relationship has terminated rather than severing all ties when he is let go. (Bonham v. Dresser Industries, Inc., CA 3-1977, 16 FEP Cases 510)	The Third Circuit also made a number of other rulings in Bonham. They included: ● 180-day period for filing notice of intent to sue does not begin to run until (1) the employee knows, or as a reasonable person should know, that the employer has made a final decision to terminate him, and (2) the employee ceases to render any further services to the employee. ● The requirement that a notice of intent to sue be filed with the Secretary of Labor within 180 days after the alleged discriminatory act is in the nature of a statute of limitations, rather than a jurisdictional prerequisite for filing an ADEA action.
	The 180-day period within which an employee is required to file a notice of intent to sue with the Secretary of Labor under ADEA began to run for an employee alleging a discriminatory demotion on the effective date of the demotion where the employee had knowledge of both the effective date of the demotion and facts that	Overruling its earlier decisions, the en banc Sixth Circuit decided that the 180-day or 300-day period for filing the notice of intent to sue is not a jurisdictional prerequisite to an ADEA action. The only jurisdictional prerequisite, it said, is giving the Secretary of Labor 60 days' notice before filing the action. The court relied

Issue	Holding	Comment
Procedures: Notice of Intent to Sue—Contd.	reasonably would have led him to conclude that the demotion was discriminatorily based. The employee's uncertainty as to whether the employer would reinstate him did not alter the date of the occurrence of the alleged unlawful action. However, the employer improperly was granted a summary judgment on the basis that the employee had not filed a timely notice of intent to sue, since genuine issues of fact existed as to whether the employer misrepresented its intent to reinstate the employee, whether he reasonably relied on this misrepresentation, and when he reasonably discovered that the employer had misrepresented its intent. One member of the three-judge panel concurred in part and dissented in part. (Coke v. General Adjustment Bureau, CA 5-1980, 22 FEP Cases 1352)	on the Dartt, Bonham, and Coke decisions, among others. (Wright v. State of Tennessee, CA 6-1980, 23 FEP Cases 714)
Procedures: State Proceeding—Commencement	Section 14(b) of the Age Discrimination in Employment Act (ADEA), like Section 706(b) of Title VII, requires a claimant to resort to appropriate state administrative proceedings before bringing an ADEA action, since (1) ADEA and Title VII share a common purpose—elimination of discrimination in the workplace; (2) language of Section 14(b) is almost identical to that of Section 706(b); and (3) legislative history of Section 14(b) indicates that its source was Section 706(b). The ADEA permits concurrent rather than sequential state and federal administrative jurisdiction in order to expedite processing of age discrimination claims, and this purpose would not be frustrated by a requirement that claimants pursue state and federal administrative remedies simultaneously. The decision was by a five-to-four margin, with Chief Justice Burger and Justices Stevens, Powell, and Rehnquist concurring in part and dissenting in part. The dissent contended that the plaintiff concededly never resorted to appropriate state remedies. This means his federal suit should not have been brought and should be dismissed. (Oscar Mayer & Co. v. Evans, US SupCt-1979, 19 FEP Cases 1167)	On the point raised by the dissent, the majority took the position that a state proceeding is commenced for deferral purposes as soon as the administrative complaint is filed, even if the complaint is untimely under state law. The requirement that a claimant "commence" state proceedings before seeking relief under ADEA, the majority said, does not require as a precondition for maintaining an ADEA action that the claimant commence those proceedings within the time set forth in the state law. Among other things, the use of the word "commence" strongly implies that the state limitation periods are irrelevant.
		The original ADEA required an aggrieved person to file a "notice of intent to sue" with the Secretary within 180 days after the alleged act of discrimination (or 300 days if a claim was filed with a state authority having the

Issue	Holding	Comment
Procedures: State Proceeding—Commencement—Contd.		power to grant or seek relief for age discrimination). The 1978 amendments changed the requirement of "a notice of intent to sue" to a requirement that the aggrieved person file "a charge" with the Secretary. In a case decided after the Supreme Court's decision, the Ninth Circuit held that a former employee who filed a notice of intent to sue 229 days after his alleged unlawful termination may sue the employer under ADEA, even though he failed to file a timely claim with the state FEP agency. The court said that an ADEA claimant may provide notice of intent to sue within 300 days of the alleged discrimination in a deferral state regardless of whether state procedures have been commenced timely; the Act requires only that the state proceedings commence 60 days before an action is brought in a federal court. (Bean v. Crocker National Bank, CA 9-1979, 20 FEP Cases 533) But see Eklund v. Lubrizol Corp., CA 6-1976, 12 FEP Cases 367, in which the court rejected the plaintiff's contention that the 300-day provision, rather than the 180-day provision was applicable. It found that the state agency was not authorized to seek relief from discriminatory practices and so was not a deferral state.
Procedures: State Proceedings—Government Actions	Although private persons who want to pursue their rights under ADEA have to file with a state agency concerned with age discrimination, if there is one, before they may seek relief in federal court under the federal law, the Secretary of Labor does not have to follow the same procedure before bringing a lawsuit in his own name. A lawsuit brought by the Secretary, unlike a lawsuit brought by a private person, is not brought under Section 7 of ADEA in any real sense. Instead, it derives from the Fair Labor Standards Act, and the FLSA does not require the Secretary to resort to state administrative procedures before suing. (Marshall v. Chamberlain Mfg. Co., CA 3-1979, 20 FEP Cases 147)	This was the first appellate court ruling on the question, and it has a limiting effect on the holding in Oscar Mayer & Co., v. Evans, supra. The court said there is no indication that Congress intended that the Secretary resort to state administrative remedies before suing under ADEA.
Procedures: Statute of Limitations—Employer Misrepresentations	A former employee who claimed that he did not file an action under the Age Discrimination in Employment Act (ADEA) within the required three-year period for willful violations because of misrepresentations by the employer is entitled to a jury trial to determine whether the	After holding that the trial court improperly granted the employer's motion for summary judgment, the court turned to whether the issue of equitable estoppel was triable by a jury. It decided that a jury should resolve whether the consultation agreement consti-

Issue	Holding	Comment
Procedures: Statute of Limitations—Employer Misrepresentations—Contd.	limitations period should be tolled and, if so, to what extent. The former employee asserted that the employer falsely induced him to accept a consultation agreement calling for his early retirement and that he did not discover the employer's true position until after the statute of limitations had run. (Ott v. Midland-Ross Corp., CA 6-1979, 19 FEP Cases 1465)	tuted a wrongful inducement for the former employee to forego his rights under the ADEA.

Title VII, Civil Rights Act of 1964

Issue	Holding	Comment
Civil Rights Act, Title VII: Procedures Aggrieved Person	To be an "aggrieved person" entitled to bring an action under Title VII, it is not necessary to be an "employee." In one case, the U.S. Court of Appeals for the Third Circuit held that a "pensioner" was an "aggrieved person" entitled to sue under Title VII. (Hackett v. McGuire Bros., Inc., CA 3-1971, 3 FEP Cases 648)	Another appeals court—that for the Fifth Circuit—ruled that males who had not made application for the position of airline stewardess were "aggrieved persons" within the meaning of Title VII. The court said they were effectively deterred by an ad seeking females for the position and so reasonably could believe that it was futile for them to file an application. (Hailes v. United Airlines, CA 5-1972, 4 FEP Cases 1022)
Attorneys' Fees: Award to Defendant—Private Employer	A federal district court exercised its discretion squarely within the permissible bounds of Section 706(k) of Title VII when it denied the award of attorneys' fees to an employer that prevailed in an action brought against it by the EEOC. The court found that the EEOC did not act unreasonably because the basis on which the employer prevailed was an issue of first impression requiring judicial resolution and because the EEOC's interpretation of the disputed statutory provision was not frivolous. The issue related to whether the EEOC could sue on a charge that was not pending before the 1972 amendments took effect, which gave the EEOC the right to sue. The decision was unanimous, with Justice Blackmun not participating. (Christiansburg Garment Co. v. EEOC, US SupCt-1978, 16 FEP Cases 502)	The court said the general standard for assessing attorneys' fees against the EEOC when it loses a Title VII action is not different from the standard applicable to private parties who bring a losing Title VII action, although the district court may consider distinctions between the EEOC and private plaintiffs in determining the reasonableness of the EEOC's litigation efforts. A federal district court, the Supreme Court said, may award attorneys' fees to a prevailing defendant in a Title VII action upon a finding that the action was frivolous, unreasonable, or without foundation, even though not brought in subjective bad faith.
	Although Title VII provides for awards of attorneys' fees to either plaintiff or defendants, awards against private plaintiffs to prevailing defendants are not the general rule, in view of the congressional priority given to vindicating the rights of complaining employees and the likelihood that their need for financial assistance will be greater than that of the defendants. (Richardson v. Hotel Corp. of America, USDC ELa-1971, 3 FEP Cases 1031; Miller v. International Paper Co., CA 5-1969, 1 FEP Cases 647)	To discourage "frivolous" suits, however, courts have ordered employees bringing such suits to pay the attorneys' fees of unions and employers that the courts said were unjustly charged with discrimination. (See Matyi v. Beer Bottlers, USDC EMo-1974, 9 FEP Cases 48; Robinson v. KMOX-TV, USDC EMo-1975, 11 FEP Cases 465)

Issue	Holding	Comment
Civil Rights Act, Title VII: Procedures—Contd. Attorneys' Fees: Award to Defendant—Private Employer—Contd.	Attorneys' fees awarded to a successful defendant in an action brought under Title VII should not exceed what is necessary to fulfill the deterrence provision without subjecting the plaintiff to financial ruin. The district court had approved an award of $2,500 in attorneys' fees, but the Second Circuit reduced the amount to $120 for the employer and $80 for the union in view of the limited income and finances of the plaintiff. (Faraci v. Hickey-Freeman, Inc., CA 2-1979, 20 FEP Cases 1777)	The district court found that the plaintiff's action was a "frivolous lawsuit maliciously filed" and so came under the rule laid down in Christiansburg Garment Co. v. EEOC, supra, permitting assessment of attorneys' fees against a losing plaintiff where the claim is "frivolous, unreasonable, or groundless."
Attorneys' Fees: Award to Defendant—Private Employer, Bad Faith	Federal Courts have an inherent power to assess attorneys' fees against a party who is found to have litigated in bad faith. This power includes the authority to force an attorney who willfully abuses the judicial process to pay such additional expenses incurred by the other side. The holding stemmed from a determination by a federal district court that three lawyers who handled an employment discrimination case were guilty of misconduct that substantially increased the costs of the employer's defense. Justice Powell wrote an opinion in which Justices Stewart and Rehnquist joined in all but the discussion of the court's inherent disciplinary powers—an issue which they find should be discussed in the first instance by the trial judge on remand. Justice Blackmun joined in the remand based on Justice Powell's discussion of Section 37(b) of the Federal Rules of Civil Procedure dealing with sanctions for failure to comply with discovery orders and the court's inherent disciplinary powers over attorneys. Justice Stevens approved of the circuit court's interpretation of the U.S.C. Sec. 1927 and also dissented to the discussion by the majority of the court's inherent disciplinary powers over attorneys. Chief Justice Burger, also dissenting, would have reinstated the trial judge's original order. (Roadway Express Inc. v. Piper, US SupCt-1980, 23 FEP Cases 12)	The case involved a class action alleging employment discrimination based on race. The trial court found that the three attorneys who handled the suit for the plaintiffs were responsible for misconduct that substantially increased the costs of the employer's defense. It dismissed the suit and ordered the three attorneys to pay the employer $17,372.53 to cover its expenses. The Fifth Circuit held that the attorneys could be required to pay the employer's costs, but not its attorneys' fees. (Monk v. Roadway Express, USDC WLa-1977, 20 FEP Cases 583; CA 5-1979, 20 FEP Cases 588)
Attorneys' Fees: Award to Defendant—Private Employer, Frivolous Action	An employer that was required to continue litigating former black employee's Title VII action until a federal district court granted its motion for dismissal is entitled to an award of attorney's fees for time spent litigating the motion after the former employee's counsel received a copy of the motion, which contained a release that former employee had signed and	

Issue	Holding	Comment
Civil Rights Act, Title VII: Procedures—Contd.	that barred his claim. Counsel could have concluded on receipt of the motion that the action was frivolous, but because of his refusal to react, the case was unduly prolonged. (Davis v. Braniff Airways, USDC NTex-1979, 19 FEP Cases 811)	
Attorneys' Fees: Award to Defendant—U.S. Government Employer	A U.S. Government employee who brought an action against her agency in bad faith may be assessed attorneys' fees to be awarded to the defendant, even though Section 706(k) of Title VII excludes the EEOC and the United States from collecting attorneys' fees if they are the prevailing parties. An award of attorneys' fees in such cases will deter abusive litigation in the future. The legislative history and the underlying purposes of Section 706(k) indicate that Congress left undisturbed the historical discretion of a federal district court to award attorneys' fees to deter the bringing of actions without foundation. The social benefits of deterring Title VII actions against the U.S. Government by awarding it attorneys' fees outweigh the social costs arising from the risk that some meritorious actions will be discouraged. (Copeland v. Martinez, CA DC-1979, 20 FEP Cases 330)	The courts quoted from the Supreme Court's opinion in Christiansburg Garment Co. v. EEOC, supra, to the effect that the purpose of Section 706(k) was to "make it easier for a plaintiff of limited means to bring a meritorious suit." It added that while Congress wanted to clear the way for suits to be brought under the Act, it also wanted to protect defendants from burdensome litigation having no legal or factual basis.
Award to Plaintiff: Private Employer	A federal district court abused its discretion in awarding attorney's fees to individuals who brought a successful Title VII action where its award (1) does not elucidate factors on which it was based, (2) does not show any correlation to facts and figures submitted by individuals, (3) does not match local minimum fee scale, (4) does not differentiate between experienced and inexperienced attorneys representing individuals, and (5) leaves unexplained disallowance of between 239.5 to 299.5 of hours claimed. In so ruling, the Fifth Circuit said that an individual bringing a Title VII action has the burden of proving his entitlement to attorneys' fees just as he would bear the burden of proving a claim for any other money judgment. (Johnson v. Georgia Highway Express, CA 5-1974, 7 FEP Cases 1)	In its opinion, the court listed the following guidelines of determining awards of attorneys' fees to individuals who bring successful Title VII actions. ● The time and labor required. Although hours spent or claimed should not be the sole basis for determing a fee, they are a necessary ingredient to be considered. ● The novelty and difficulty of the questions. Cases of first impression generally require more time and effort. ● The skill requisite to perform the legal service properly. ● The preclusion of other employment by the attorney due to acceptance of the case. ● The customary fee for similar work in the community. ● Whether the fee is fixed or contingent. ● Time limitations opposed by the client or the circumstances. ● Priority work that delays the lawyer's other legal work is entitled to some premium. ● The amounts involved and the results

Issue	Holding	Comment
Civil Rights Act, Title VII: Procedures—Contd. Award to Plaintiff: Private Employer—Contd.		obtained. ● The experience, reputation, and ability of the attorneys. ● The undesirability of the case. Civil rights attorneys fact hardships in their communities because of their desire to help the civil rights litigant. ● The nature and length of the professional relationship with the client. ● Awards in similar cases within the court's circuit and outside it. In a case decided shortly after, the D.C. Circuit aligned itself with the Fifth Circuit and adopted the same guidelines for determining attorneys's fees in suits brought by individuals under Title VII. (Evans v. Sheraton Park Hotel, CA DC-1974, 8 FEP Cases 705)
	The award by a federal district court of $15,000 in attorneys' fees to a lawyer who successfully appealed an adverse decision in an action under Title VII was not an abuse of discretion by the court. The attorney claimed to have spent 585 hours in handling the appeal and the remand of the case to the district court. The appeals court also pointed out that the district court judge who determined the fee was a experienced trial lawyer accustomed to the manifest difficulties in fixing reasonable attorneys' fees. (Weeks v. Southern Bell Telephone & Telegraph Co., CA 5-1972, 4 FEP Cases 1255)	The decision was by a three-judge panel consisting of Wisdom and Thornberry, circuit judges, and Smith, district judge. Judge Wisdom dissented, taking the position that the difficulty of the case may have warranted a higher fee and recommending that the case be remanded to the district court for reconsideration of the reasonableness of the fee.
	A federal district court did not abuse its discretion when it awarded $10,000 in attorneys' fees to 12 lawyers who brought a successful action under Title VII and who claimed to have spent 515 hours in handling the action. In holding that the fee was within the bounds of reasonableness, the court noted the number of lawyers involved, indications of duplication of effort, the trial judge's view that some of the work reasonably would have required less time than actually was spent on it, and the trial judge's observation of the lawyers' product and his capacity to evaluate it. (Lea v. Cone Mills Corp., CA 4-1972, 4 FEP Cases 1259)	The decision was by a panel consisting of Chief Judge Haynsworth, Circuit Judge Winter, and District Judge Young. Judge Winter dissented. In his view, the fee should have been computed at a rate of $40 an hour, and the total fee to the termination of the litigation should have been $25,000.
Attorneys' Fees: Denial of Award—Lack of Relief	No attorneys' fees should be awarded to a retired school teacher who proved that she had been discriminated against in working condi-	The purpose behind the provision in Title VII for the award of attorneys' fees to successful litigants was to encourage lawyers to take

Issue	Holding	Comment
Civil Rights Act, Title VII: Procedures—Contd. Attorneys' Fees: Denial of Award—Lack of Relief—Contd.	tions because of her sex. The teacher did not obtain an injunction or back pay, and Title VII does not permit her to recover compensatory damages for the discriminatory treatment. In addition to the discriminatory working conditions charge, the teacher alleged that she was discriminated against with regard to her salary and that she was constructively discharged. The trial court rejected the salary and constructive discharge claims, but found that the teacher had been required to work under conditions that were inferior to those of male teachers. It also found that she was not entitled to back pay and that she could not be reinstated because of a physical disability. Because the teacher had not obtained back pay, reinstatement, or injunctive relief, she was not a prevailing party who may be awarded attorneys' fees, the appeals court said. To be a prevailing party, the court added, a plaintiff must have been entitled to some form of relief at the time the suit was brought. It was apparent that the plaintiff teacher was not entitled to such relief. To award attorneys' fees to a litigant who was not entitled to any relief at the time the lawsuit was brought, the court concluded, would only serve to encourage fruitless litigation. (Harrington v. Vandalia-Butler Board of Education, CA 6-1978, 18 FEP Cases 348)	employment discrimination cases. At the time a suit is filed, it often is not known whether the plaintiff would be entitled to relief even if he made out a case. So the decision in this case, if accepted by other courts, could result in fewer challenges to apparently unlawful practices in working conditions that cannot be compensated for by monetary relief.
Attorneys' Fees: Denial of Award—Prevailing Party	Section 706(k) of Title VII authorizes the courts to award attorneys' fees to the "prevailing party" in a Title VII suit. But what is a "prevailing party"? In a leading case on this issue, the D.C. Circuit held that an employee who had prevailed on an interlocutory appeal from an order requiring her to exhaust administrative remedies before proceeding further with her Title VII action was not entitled to attorneys' fees because she had not yet proved discrimination and so was not the prevailing party within Section 706(k). The court found her claim premature. (Grubbs v. Butz, CA DC-1976, 13 FEP Cases 245)	In a case decided by the Ninth Circuit, an employer that prevailed on EEOC's interlocutory appeal from a federal district court order limiting EEOC's intervention in a Title VII action was held to be a "prevailing party" within the meaning of Section 706(k), and therefore was eligible for award of attorneys' fees connected with the appeal, even though the employer may not prevail in the principal case. The interlocutory appeal was sufficiently significant and discrete to be treated as a separate unit. The court added that the employer's ability to pay its own way is not necessarily a bar to the award of attorneys' fees. (Van Hoomissen v. Xerox Corp., CA 9-1974, 8 FEP Cases 725)
Attorneys' Fees: Federal Employment	A federal district court has discretion to award attorneys' fees that include compensation for legal services performed at both judicial and administrative levels in a Title VII action in	In a later case, a federal district court held that a U.S. Government agency has authority under Title VII to award attorneys' fees to complainants who prevail before it and receive

Issue	Holding	Comment
Civil Rights Act, Title VII: Procedures—Contd.	which a U.S. Government employee is the prevailing party. (Parker v. Califano, CA DC-1977, 18 FEP Cases 391)	from it the complete relief requested. (Smith v. Califano, USDC DC-1978, 18 FEP Cases 657) Also see Fischer v. Adams, CA 1-1978, 18 FEP Cases 667, in which a court awarded attorneys' fees to a government employee.
Attorneys' Fees: Federal Employment—Contd.	The method of calculating the amount of attorneys' fees in a Title VII action against the U.S. Government should not differ from the method of calculating an award against a private defendant, the D.C. Circuit held. It rejected the proposal of a dissenting judge who argued that a "cost plus" approach should be used to prevent the attorneys for a prevailing plaintiff from obtaining an unreasonable profit. Instead, the court said that a "lodestar" fee, based on hours spent on issues on which the plaintiff prevailed and the hourly rate, should be calculated first. That "lodestar" fee should then be adjusted to take account of such items as risk that no fee would be obtained and unusually good or bad representation. The court found it immaterial that the law firm who represented the plaintiff planned to donate its fee award to a "public interest" law entity. (Copeland v. Marshall, CA DC-1980, 23 FEP Cases 967)	
Attorneys' Fees: State Action	Section 706(k) of Title VII, which authorizes the award of attorneys' fees to the prevailing party in "any" action "or proceeding under this title," enables the charging party to recover attorneys' fees for legal work done in state administrative and judicial proceedings to which she was referred pursuant to the enforcement scheme of Title VII. Since it is clear that Congress intended to authorize fee awards for work done in administrative proceedings, authorization for private actions in Section 7(b)(1) of Act encompasses an action solely to obtain attorneys' fees for work in state and local proceedings. Justice Blackmun wrote the opinion of the Court. Justices White and Rehnquist dissented. Chief Justice Burger joined in the opinion with the exception of one footnote; Justice Stevens concurred. (New York Gaslight Club v. Carey, US SupCt-1980, 22 FEP Cases 1642)	On a constitutional issue, the Court also ruled that the power of Congress under Section 5 of the Fourteenth Amendment overrides any interest that the state might have in not authorizing attorneys' fees for legal work done in connection with state FEP proceedings, notwithstanding a contention that such an award infringes on the states powers under the Tenth Amendment.

Issue	Holding	Comment
Back-Pay Awards	Once a court has found that Title VII of the Civil Rights Act of 1964 has been violated, back pay should be denied only for reasons that, if applied generally, would not frustrate the central purposes of Title VII of eradicating discrimination throughout the economy and making persons whole for injuries suffered through past discrimination. If a federal district court declines to award back pay, it should articulate its reasons carefully. The U.S. Supreme Court so ruled in vacating and remanding a case in which a district court decided that no back pay should be awarded to any member of a class, though at least some members of the class suffered loss of wage opportunities because of an unlawfully discriminatory system of job seniority. The decision was reversed by the U.S. Court of Appeals for the Fourth Circuit. (Moody v. Albemarle Paper Co., USDC ENC-1971, 4 FEP Cases 561; Moody v. Albemarle Paper Co., CA 4-1973, 5 FEP Cases 613) The Supreme Court in an opinion by Justice Stewart held that the lack of bad faith on the part of the employer is not a sufficient reason for denying back pay to discriminatees, but a denial may be justified on the ground of laches. (Albemarle Paper Co. v. Moody, US SupCt-1975, 10 FEP Cases 1181) See below under "Substantive Rulings: Ability Tests" for discussion of another issue in the case.	The courts also have upheld the right of the Attorney General to seek back pay in a pattern-or-practice action under Section 707 of the Act. (See U.S. v. Georgia Power Co., CA 5-1973, 5 FEP Cases 587; U.S. v. Lee Way Motor Freight, USDC WOkla-1973, 7 FEP Cases 710) Prior to the Supreme Court's decision, some courts had applied a good-faith standard in deciding whether to award back pay. In one case, for example, the violation by the employer was based on his good-faith attempt to comply with a state law limiting the number of hours female employees could work during a week. (LeBlanc v. Southern Bell Telephone and Telegraph Co., CA 5-1972, 4 FEP Cases 818, cert. denied by US SupCt-1972, 5 FEP Cases 149; see also U.S. v. St. Louis San Francisco Railway Co., CA 8-1972, 4 FEP Cases 853, cert. denied by US SupCt-1973, 5 FEP Cases 299; Manning v. General Motors Corp., CA 6-1972, 4 FEP Cases 1282, cert. denied by US SupCt-1973, 5 FEP Cases 587)
	Back pay may be awarded under Title VII of the Civil Rights Act of 1964 to employees who, without having filed a charge with the EEOC or having obtained notice of right to sue, intervened in other workers' action that subsequently was denied class action status. The employees who intervened were situated exactly the same as the others insofar as the alleged discrimination was concerned and the intervenors were members of the same class as the other employees. (Wheeler v. American Home Product Corp., CA 5-1977, 16 FEP 157)	The district court that tried the case had denied a motion to certify the action as a class action and had approved a settlement that provided for dismissal of the action, including the claims of the employees who had intervened and had not signed the settlement agreement. The appeals court held that the district dourt was not authorized to approve the settlement agreement.
Burden of Proof: Intentional Violation—Equal Protection Clause.	Proof of racially discriminating intent is necessary to establish violation of the Equal Protection Clause of the Fifth Amendment to the U.S. Constitution and Section 1981 U.S.C. (Civil Rights Act of 1866). So personnel tests that	As part of the rationale for the holding, the majority stated that the black applicants who failed the test could no more successfully claim that the test deprived them of equal protection than could white applicants who

Issue	Holding	Comment
Civil Rights Act, Title VII: Procedures—Contd. Burden of Proof: Intentional Violation—Equal Protection Clause.—Contd.	excluded a disproportionately large number of black applicants for police officer positions with the District of Columbia did not violate the Equal Protection Clause solely because of its racially disproportionate impact. In deciding that there was a violation of the Equal Protection Clause, the court of appeals applied statutory standards elucidated in a case under Title VII, declaring that lack of discriminatory intent in designing and administering the test was irrelevant. This is not the constitutional rule, the Supreme Court said. It has never held that the constitutional standard for adjudicating claims of invidious racial discrimination is identical to the standards applicable under Title VII. Justice Stevens concurred, and Justice Stewart joined in only part of the opinion. Justices Brennan and Marshall dissented. (Washington v. Davis, US SupCt-1976, 12 FEP Cases 1415)	also failed the test, even in the face of proof that more blacks than whites has been disqualified by the test. The Court also said the district courts' "correct" holding that affirmative efforts of the police department to recruit black officers, the changing racial composition of the recruit classes and of the police force in general, and the relationship of the test to the training program negated any inference that the police department discriminated on the basis of race. About the test itself, the Court stated that the district court's conclusion that performance in the training course was sufficient to validate the test was supported by regulations of the U.S. Civil Service Commission and by the current views of the Civil Service Commissioners who were parties to the case challenging the test—wholly aside from the relationship of the test to actual performance as a police officer.
Burden of Proof: Intentional Violation—Title VII	Proof of intentional violation is not essential in Title VII action even when the employer-defendant is a government agency and even assuming that Title VII was enacted pursuant to Congress' power under the Fourteenth Amendment alone. Congress is authorized to enact more stringent standards than those provided by the Fourteenth and Fifteenth Amendments to carry out the purpose of those amendments, and Title VII is unquestionably appropriate legislation to enforce the Equal Protection of the Laws Clause. The case involved tests used by the City in hiring, which the court found had a disparate impact on black employees. The court found further that the City failed to show that the tests were validated and that the evidence casts doubt on the validity of the tests. The court added that evidence that the City sought to recruit blacks to be employees and to enhance their job opportunities was insufficient to rebute a prima facie case of racial discrimination established by statistics. (Scott v. City of Anniston, CA 5-1979, 20 FEP Cases 62)	The Court distinguished between actions brought under the Constitution and Section 1981 U.S.C. (Civil Rights Act of 1866) and those brought under Title VII with respect to proof of discriminatory intent. In Washington v. Davis, supra, the court pointed out, the Supreme Court held that to prevail under the Constitution and Section 1981, a plaintiff must prove discriminatory purpose. But in Teamsters v. U.S. (T.I.M.E.-D.C., Inc.), US SupCt-1977, 14 FEP Cases 1514), the Court reaffirmed that discriminatory intent need not be shown in a Title VII action. Moreover, the court added, both the Seventh and Eighth circuits have held that a Title VII plaintiff need not prove intentional discrimination in an action against a governmental unit. (U.S. v. City of Chicago, CA 7-1978, 16 FEP Cases 908; Firefighters Institute for Racial Equality v. City of Chicago, CA 8-1977, 14 FEP Cases 1486, cert. denied, US SupCt-1977, 15 FEP Cases 1184)
Burden of Proof: Prima Facie Case	In an action under Title VII of the Civil Rights Act of 1964, a complainant must carry the initial burden of establishing a prima facie case of racial discrimination. He may do this by showing that (1) he belongs to a racial minority, (2) he applied and was qualified for a job for	The plaintiff in this case was a former employee whom the employer refused to rehire. The court said the employer would meet its burden of successfully rebutting the former employee's claim of racial discrimination if the evidence showed, as alleged by the employer,

Issue	Holding	Comment
Civil Rights Act, Title VII: Procedures—Contd. Burden of Proof: Prima Facie Case—Contd.	which the employer was seeking applicants, (3) he was rejected despite his qualifications, and (4) the position remained open after his rejection, and the employer continued to seek applications from persons with the complainant's qualifications. The burden then shifts to the employer to articulate some legitimate nondiscriminatory reason for the complainant's rejection. (McDonnell Douglas Corp. v. Green, US SupCt-1973, 5 FEP Cases 965)	that the former employee participated in an unlawful "stall-in" designed to impede access and egress to the employer's plant at the peak traffic hour. But if this is established, the court added, the former employee must be afforded a fair opportunity to show that the employer's stated reason for rejecting him was, in fact, pretextual. This can be shown by (1) evidence that white employees involved in acts against the employer of comparable seriousness to the "stall-in" were retained or rehired, (2) facts as to the employer's treatment of the former employee during his prior term of employment, (3) the employer's reaction, if any, to the former employee's legitimate civil rights activities, and (4) the employer's general policy and practice with respect to minority-group employment.
Burden of Proof: Prima Facie Case—Rebuttal	An employer that is required to articulate some legitimate nondiscriminatory reason for the apparently unequal treatment in order to rebut a prima facie case of discrimination is not required to "prove the absence of any discriminatory motive." The Supreme Court vacated a lower court decision requiring such proof and remanded the case. The decision was by a five-to-four margin, with Justices Stevens, Brennan, Stewart, and Marshall dissenting. (Board of Trustees v. Sweeney, US SupCt-1978, 18 FEP Cases 520)	In support of its holding, the majority cited McDonnell Douglas Corp. v. Green, supra, and Furnco Construction Corp. v. Waters, supra.
	An employer's proof that its work force is racially balanced or that it contains a disproportionately high percentage of minority-group employees has some relevance to the employer's efforts to rebut a prima facie case of racial discrimination in hiring. But such proof cannot conclusively resolve the question of whether an otherwise unexplained rejection of minority-group applicants was discriminatorily motivated. Justices Brennan and Marshall concurred in part and dissented in part. (Furnco Construction Corp. v. Waters, US SupCt-1978, 17 FEP Cases 1062)	The court said that an employer seeking to rebut a prima facie case of racial discrimination in hiring must prove that its employment procedures are based on legitimate considerations, but it need not prove that these procedures allow it to consider the qualifications of the largest number of minority-group job applicants. It does not have a duty to adopt a hiring procedure that maximizes the hiring of minority-group employees. Moreover, the court added, the obligation imposed on an employer by Title VII is to provide equal opportunity for each applicant without regard to whether members of the applicant's race are already proportionately represented in the work force.

Issue	Holding	Comment
Civil Rights Act, Title VII: Procedures—Contd. Burden of Proof: Statistical Evidence, Pattern-or-Practice Action	The proper statistical comparison in a pattern-or-practice action against a school district for alleged racial discrimination in hiring practices is between the racial composition of the district's teaching staff and the racial composition of the qualified public school teacher population in the relevant labor market— not between the teaching staff and the student population. Evidence that the percentage of qualified black teachers in the area was at least three to four times the percentage of blacks on the school district's teaching staff established a prima facie case of racial discrimination by the school district. But this prima facie proof of racial discrimination may be rebutted by statistics dealing with the district's hiring after it became subject to Title VII in 1972. So the court of appeals erred in disregarding the district's post-1972 hiring statistics. The decision below was vacated and the case was remanded to the federal district court. (Hazelwood School District v. U.S., US SupCt-1977, 15 FEP Cases 1)	In addition to laying down the general rules, the court set out some considerations for the district court to evaluate in determining whether the percentage of black teachers hired by the school district should be compared with the percentage of black teachers hired by all school districts in the county, with the percentage of black teachers hired by school districts in a neighboring city that have followed a policy of attempting to maintain a 50-percent black teaching staff, or with some intermediate figure. The considerations were: (1) whether the racially-based hiring policies of the city were in effect in the year in which the census figures were taken; (2) to what extent those policies have changed the racial composition of that district's teaching staff from what it otherwise would have been; (3) to what extent the city's recruitment policies have diverted the city teachers who might otherwise have applied to the school district in question; (4) to what extent the black teachers employed by the city would prefer employment in other districts such as the school district in question; and (5) what experience in other school districts in the county indicates about the validity of excluding the neighboring city from the revelant labor market. The court added that proof that an employer engaged in racial discrimination prior to the effective date of Title VII might in some circumstances support an inference that such discrimination continued after the effective date of the Act, particularly where relevant aspects of the decision-making process had undergone little change.
	Statistics showing a racial imbalance in the composition of an employer's work force as compared with the composition of the population in the community from which employees are hired are probative in a case alleging racial discrimination in hiring by an employer. Even though Section 703(j) of the Civil Rights Act of 1964 makes clear that Title VII imposes no requirement that the work force mirror the general population, it ordinarily is to be expected, in the absence of an explanation, that nondiscriminatory hiring practices in time will result in a work force more or less representative of the racial composition of the community. However, considerations such as the small sample size and evidence that that the figures	This case was more notable for its discussion of the effect of Title VII on bona fide seniority systems. For a discussion of this aspect of the case, see "Past Discrimination: Seniority Systems" below.

Issue	Holding	Comment
Civil Rights Act, Title VII: Procedures—Contd.	for the general population might not accurately reflect the pool of qualified job applicants also would be relevant. (Teamsters v. U.S. [T.I.M.E.-D.C., Inc.], US SupCt-1977, 14 FEP Cases 1514)	
Burden of Proof: Statistical Evidence, Individual Action	Statistical evidence may establish a prima facie case of employment discrimination against an individual as well as a class. Statistical proof in a class action of a broad based policy of employment discrimination provides reasonable grounds to infer that individual employment decisions were made in pursuit of the discriminatory policy, and this use of statistical evidence should have equal force and effect in an individual discrimination case. One judge dissented. (Davis v. Califano, CA DC-1979, 21 FEP Cases 272)	There has not been any consensus as to the extent to which classified evidence should be considered probative in an action brought on behalf of an single person. The Sixth Circuit, for example, said that statistical evidence "is of much greater value in discrimination cases where large numbers of employees are involved and fewer subjective personalized factors are considered. (EEOC v. New York Times Broadcasting Service, CA 6-1976, 13 FEP Cases 813) In a case involving discharge allegedly based on race, the Eighth Circuit said that the statistical breakdown of the company's work force did not compel the conclusion that the employee was discharged because of his race. Statistical evidence of a pattern or practice of discrimination may be of probative value in an individual case to show motive, interest, or purpose, the Court said, but it is not determinative of an employer's reason for the action taken against an individual grievant. (King v. Yellow Freight System, Inc., CA 8-1975, 11 FEP Cases 867)
Burden of Proof: Statistical Evidence, Specialized Positions	General population statistics may not be used to establish a prima facie case of discrimination in specialized positions if the employer establishes that the positions require special qualifications. In this situation, there must be a comparison between the racial composition of the relevant portion of the employer's work force after the effective date of Title VII and the racial composition of qualified workers in the relevant labor market. But the burden is on the employer to establish that these jobs require special qualifications not possessed or readily acquired by the general population, at the peril of having the general population statistics presumed appropriate. (EEOC v. Radiator Specialty Co., CA 4-1979, 21 FEP Cases 351)	The lower court had found that the EEOC had established a case of discrimination by showing gross disparities between the racial composition of the employer's clerical, sales, professional, and managerial jobs and both the general population and the employer's own work force. It rejected the argument that statistics showing the percentage of blacks in various job categories are more reliable for assessing the impact of its employment practices. (EEOC v. Radiator Specialty Co., USDC NC-1978, 20 FEP Cases 704) Under the reasoning of the appeals court, the employer's statistics should not have been rejected out of hand.
Class Actions: General Rules	The federal appeals courts generally have accorded a liberal interpretation of the rules governing class actions. The Seventh Circuit, for example, said: "A suit for violation of Title	Class actions under Title VII are governed by Rule 23(a) of the Federal Rules of Civil Procedure. Rule 23(a) specifies that an action may be maintained as a class action only if *all*

Issue	Holding	Comment
Civil Rights Act, Title VII: Procedures—Contd. Class Actions: General Rules—Contd.	VII is necessarily a class action as the evil sought to be ended is discrimination on the basis of a class characteristic." It added that each member of the class need not file a charge with the EEOC. A plaintiff may bring a class action on behalf of those who have not filed a charge, and they may share in the remedial order of back pay. (Bowe v. Colgate-Palmolive Co., CA 7-1969, 2 FEP Cases 121)	the following requirements are met: ● The class is so numerous that joinder of all parties is impracticable. ● There are questions of law or fact common to the class. ● The claims or defenses of the representative parties are typical of the claim or defenses of the class. ● The representative parties will fairly and adequately protect the interest of the class. In addition to these four requirements, Rule 23(b) specifies three more requirements, one of which must be met. They are: (1) Separate actions would create a risk of inconsistent adjudications or adjudications that would substantially impair the ability of nonparties to protect their interests; (2) where injunctive relief is sought the party opposing the class has acted or refused to act on grounds generally applicable to the class; *or* (3) questions of law or fact common to members of the class predominate over questions affecting only individual members, and a class action is the superior method for fairly and efficiently adjudicating the controversy.
	In a similar ruling, the Ninth Circuit said that a suit protesting employment discrimination based on race, sex, or national origin is by definition a class action. So Rule 23, the court added, must be interpreted literally so as not to undermine the purpose and effectiveness of Title VII in eradicating class-based discrimination. (Gay v. Waiters Union, Local 30, CA 9-1977, 14 FEP Cases 995)	
Class Actions: Broad Action by EEOC	The EEOC may seek class-wide relief under Section 706(f)(1) of Title VII without complying with Rule 23 of the Federal Rules of Civil Procedure. To force actions by EEOC under Section 706 into the Rule 23 model would in many cases distort Rule 23 as it is commonly interpreted and in other cases would foreclose enforcement actions not satisfying Rule 23 standards but seemingly authorized by Section 706(f)(1). When the EEOC brings an action under Title VII, albeit at the behest of and for the benefit of specific individuals, it acts also to vindicate the public interest in preventing employment discrimination. The Court added that an approach that permits the EEOC to allege	The decision affirmed that of the Ninth Circuit. (EEOC v. General Telephone Co. of the Northwest, CA 9-1979, 20 FEP Cases 52) The dissenting Justices stated they would hold otherwise for the reasons stated by the Fifth Circuit in EEOC v. D.H. Holmes Co., CA 5-1977, 15 FEP Cases 378, cert. denied by US SupCt-1978, 17 FEP Cases 1000.

Issue	Holding	Comment
Civil Rights Act, Title VII: Procedures—Contd.	any violations that it discovers in the course of a reasonable investigation of the charging party's charge is far more consistent with the EEOC's role in enforcing Title VII than that of imposing the strictures of Rule 23, which would limit the EEOC action to claims typified by those of the charging party. The decision was by a five-to-four margin, with Chief Justice Burger and Justices Powell, Rehnquist, and Stevens dissenting. (General Telephone Co. of the Northwest v. EEOC, US SupCt-1980, 22 FEP Cases 1196)	
Class Actions: Dismissal of Individual Action	A Title VII action filed by a former employee who raised both individual and class claims still could be maintained as a class action even after a federal district court found that his individual claim was without merit. The district court erred when it dismissed the class claim upon finding that the former employee was not a member of the class. The court should decide whether the former employee has a link with the class and its interests and claims within the meaning of the Federal Rule of Civil Procedure. If so, the former employee should be permitted to maintain the class action even though he lost his individual claim. (Huff v. Cass Co., CA 5-1973, 6 FEP Cases 400)	The decision was made upon a rehearing by the court en banc. A panel of the court earlier had held by a margin of two-to-one that both the individual and the class action should be dismissed. (Huff v. Cass Co., CA 5-1972, 4 FEP Cases 741)
Class Actions: Filing of Charge	Persons charging unlawful job discrimination may bring a class action under Title VII, and it is not necessary for each member to have filed a charge with the EEOC. On this ground, the Fifth Circuit reinstated as plaintiffs several blacks who had been eliminated from the action because they had not sought relief through the EEOC. Participation by the class members was limited, however, to those issues that could be raised by the black employee who did file a charge with EEOC. (Oatis v. Crown Zellerbach Corp., CA 5-1968, 68 LRRM 2782, 1 FEP Cases 328)	
	But the Fifth Circuit held later that the issues would not be limited to those raised by the plaintiff if the action was filed under both Title VII and the 1866 Act, 42 U.S.C. Sec. 1981, (Alpha Portland Cement Co., v. Reese CA 5-1975, 10 FEP Cases 126)	

Issue	Holding	Comment
Civil Rights Act, Title VII: Procedures—Contd. Class Actions: Lack of Nexus with Class	A female rejected job applicant would not be an adequate representative of a class of city employees where she neither alleged in her complaint nor proved at trial any facts indicating that she herself has been injured or will be injured by any of the city's policies of which she complains other than those relating to a claim now shown to be untenable. Because she was not a victim of discrimination, she is not a present member of the class, and she was not a member even at the time of the filing of the action. This lack of nexus and the lack of merit to her individual claim is what proves that she is not a proper class representative. (Satterwhite v. City of Greenville, CA 5-1978, 17 FEP Cases 1451)	In making its decision, the Fifth Circuit relied on language in the Supreme Court's Rodriguez opinion to the effect that "a class representative must be part of the class and possess the same interests and suffer the same injury as the class members." (East Texas Motor Freight System, Inc. v. Rodriguez, US SupCt-1977, 14 FEP Cases 1508)
Class Actions: Limitation of Class	A class action filed under Title VII properly was limited to the class of black employees employed at the company's frozen food warehouse in Denver, Colorado. In so ruling, the Tenth Circuit adopted a restrictive interpretation of Rule 23(a)(3) of the Federal Rules of Civil Procedure that the "claims or defenses of the representative parties be typical of the claims or defenses of the class." (Taylor v. Safeway Stores, Inc., CA 10-1975, 11 FEP Cases 449)	In a case involving several airlines, the Seventh Circuit held that the Stewards and Stewardesses Union was not an adequate representative of a class of former stewardesses protesting a policy of terminating pregnant stewardesses and so could not settle class actions brought against the airlines by present and former stewardesses. One requirement for reinstatement was that the stewardesses pass a weight test. (Stewards v. American Airlines, CA 7-1973, 6 FEP Cases 1197)
Class Actions: Pleading of Action	Class relief was granted to all airline stewardesses who have been terminated under a no-marriage rule found to be illegal. The Seventh Circuit held that class relief could be granted even if the suit was not pleaded as class action. (Sprogis v. United Air Lines, Inc., CA 7-1971, 3 FEP Cases 621; cert. denied by US SupCt-1971, 4 FEP Cases 37)	The Fifth Circuit, however, held in another case that if a case was not pleaded as a class action, the plaintiff could not obtain class relief. (Danner v. Phillips Petroleum Co., CA 5-1971, 3 FEP Cases 858; see also Nance v. Union Carbide Corp., CA 4-1976, 13 FEP Cases 231)
Class Actions: Notice of Action	An absent member of a class of black employees who was never given notice that an action challenging the employer's promotion policies was pending is not barred from maintaining his own action seeking monetary relief from the employer for allegedly denying him a promotion because of his race. Due process requires such notice before the judgment in the prior action may act as a bar. (Johnson v. General Motors Corp., CA 5-1979, 20 FEP Cases 239)	In the previous lawsuit, black employees challenged, on behalf of all black present and future employees in hourly rated jobs, the employer's procedure for selecting hourly employees to be foremen. Only injunctive relief was sought. Although the lawsuit never was formally certified as a class action, a federal district court and the Fifth Circuit both regarded it as a class action and referred to the class in the manner defined by the employees bringing the action. The Fifth Circuit found the employer's procedures unlawful, and the

Issue	Holding	Comment
Civil Rights Act, Title VII: Procedures—Contd.		district court entered a final decree intended to operate with respect to the class of employees described in the court's opinion. (Rowe v. General Motors Corp., CA 5-1972, 4 FEP Cases 445) The claim of the employee in the Johnson case, like that raised in the Rowe case, was that the employer discriminated against blacks in promotions. The only difference in the actions was that in the Johnson case the employee sought monetary relief.
Conciliation By EEOC	In a case decided after the 1972 amendments, the Eighth Circuit Court of Appeals held that the EEOC's failure to follow its regulation requiring it to give notice of the termination of conciliation efforts to an employer who had refused to participate in conciliation of proceedings warranted dismissal of EEOC's Title VII action against the employer. (EEOC v. Hickey-Mitchell Co., CA 8-1974, 8 FEP Cases 1281)	In support of its holding, the court gave the following reasons: (1) The EEOC regulation affords even the most uncooperative and recalcitrant respondent the right to be told that it has one last chance to attempt conciliation; (2) in view of the central role of conciliation in the enforcement of Title VII, it cannot be said that the regulation is merely "technical"; and (3) it cannot be concluded that the employer was not prejudiced by the EEOC's breach of its regulation, since compliance with the regulation may well give pause to the most recalcitrant employer. The case was brought by the EEOC after the 1972 amendments gave it the right to bring a court action against an alleged offender if it has been unable to secure from the respondent a conciliation agreement acceptable to the Commission.
	In the first case in which the 1972 amendments, giving the EEOC authority to bring suits in federal district courts to enforce Title VII, were applied, a district court held that the Commission must pursue efforts to eliminate alleged unlawful practices by conference, conciliation, and persuasion before filing an action in court. (EEOC v. Container Corporation of America, USDC MFla-1972, 5 FEP Cases 108) The EEOC filed an amended complaint alleging that it carried out the required procedures. But another federal district court later held that the EEOC, which alleged in its complaint that "all conditions precedent to the institution of this lawsuit have been fulfilled," must at least allege that it has been unable to obtain an acceptable conciliation agreement from the defendant employer. (EEOC v. Guaranty Savings & Loan Assn., USDC NAla-1973, 6 FEP Cases 924) But see holding in Western Electric case under heading "Finding of Reasonable Cause."	Prior to the Container holding, however, another federal district court had held that it was not necessary to go through the processes of conference, conciliation, and persuasion where a "pattern or practice" action was filed by the Justice Department. (U.S. v. Philadelphia Electric Co., USDC EPa-1972, 5 FEP Cases 261)

Issue	Holding	Comment
Civil Rights Act, Title VII: Procedures—Contd. Conciliation By EEOC—Contd.	Before the 1972 amendments, a number of courts had held that conciliation efforts by the EEOC were not a jurisdictional prerequisite to the maintenance of a Title VII suit by an aggrieved individual. The Act, the courts said, merely required that the EEOC have an opportunity to persuade the employer before the action may be brought. This rule was laid down in three cases decided by the U.S. Court of Appeals at Richmond that later were denied review by the Supreme Court. (Gaston County Dyeing Machine Co. v. Brown, CA 4-1968, 70 LRRM 3065, 1 FEP Cases 702, cert. denied by US SupCt-1969, 70 LRRM 3062, 1 FEP Cases 699; Observer Transportation Co. v. Lee, CA 4-1968, 70 LRRM 3065, 1 FEP Cases 702, cert. denied by US SupCt-1969, 70 LRRM 3062, 1 FEP Cases 699; Pilot Freight Carriers, Inc. v. Walker, CA 4-1968, 69 LRRM 2916, 1 FEP Cases 456, cert. denied by US SupCt-1969, 70 LRRM 3062, 2 FEP Cases 699)	Similar decisions were handed down by the U.S. Courts of Appeals at Philadelphia, New Orleans, and Chicago. (IBEW v. EEOC, CA 3-1968, 68 LRRM 2939, 1 FEP Cases 335; Dent v. St. Louis-San Francisco Ry., CA 5-1969, 70 LRRM 2284, 1 FEP Cases 583; Choate v. Caterpillar Tractor Co., CA 7-1968, 69 LRRM 2486, 1 FEP Cases 431) In two earlier cases, also denied review by the Supreme Court, the U.S. Court of Appeals at Richmond held that the filing of a charge with the EEOC is a prerequisite to bringing a suit under Title VII. (Stebbins v. Nationwide Mutual Insurance Co., CA 4-1967, 66 LRRM 2133, 1 FEP Cases 235, cert. denied by US SupCt-1968, 1 FEP Cases 300; Mickel v. South Carolina State Employment Service, CA 4-1967, 65 LRRM 2328, 1 FEP Cases 182, cert. denied by US SupCt-1967, 67 LRRM 2898, 1 FEP Cases 300) While trying to remedy the charging party's individual complaint, the EEOC normally attempts to include in the conciliation agreement modifications of other employment practices to bring them into compliance with Title VII. This could include an affirmative action program. In a later case, the Fourth Circuit distinguished the case before it from Hickey-Mitchell. It found that the company involved was fairly warned that a suit might be brought, but its position was that it had no interest in conciliation. So the court concluded that an offer to attempt conciliation at the option of the company would have been futile. (EEOC v. Raymond Metal Products Co., CA 4-1976, 12 FEP Cases 38)
Consent Decrees: Validity	Consent decrees entered into by the U.S. Government, nine major steel companies, and the Steelworkers Union were lawful, according to the U.S. Court of Appeals for the Fifth Circuit. The consent decrees were challenged by various intervening parties on grounds that (1) employees were required to sign them as a condition of getting back pay and this was illegal, (2) the back pay fund was inadequate, and (3) the Government abdicated its enforcement policies under Title VII of the Civil Rights Act of 1964 and Executive Order 11246. One	The consent decrees in the steel industry were the result of a program initiated by the Justice and Labor Departments and the EEOC to eliminate alleged employment discrimination in major industries and companies. In addition to big steel, the Government has negotiated consent agreements against alleged discrimination in the trucking industry and American Telephone and Telegraph Company and its subsidiaries. See FEPM 431:73 for the text of the AT&T consent decree.

Issue	Holding	Comment
Civil Rights Act, Title VII: Procedures—Contd. Consent Decrees: Validity—Contd.	consent decree provided for immediate implementation of plantwide seniority and transfer and testing reforms, the establishment of goals and timetables for fuller utilization of women in occupations and job categories from which they had been discriminatorily excluded in the past, and a back-pay fund of $30,940,000 to be paid to minority-group and women employees injured by the discriminatory practices. Another decree required the companies to begin affirmative action programs in hiring, initial assignments, promotions, management training, and recruitment of women and minority-group members. (U.S. v. Allegheny-Ludlum Industries, CA 5-1975, 11 FEP Cases 167)	
Constitutionality: Title VII Public Sector	The 1972 amendments extending the coverage of Title VII to state and local governments are constitutional. The Eleventh Amendment to the Constitution does not bar the award under Title VII of retroactive retirement benefits and attorneys' fees to individuals who proved that a state retirement system had discriminated against them because of their sex (1) The Eleventh Amendment is limited by Section 6 of the Fourteenth Amendment, which gives Congress power to enforce the substantive provisions of the Fourteenth Amendment "by appropriate legislation"; (2) Congress may provide, in determining what is "appropriate legislation," for private actions against states or state officials that are constitutionally impermissible in other contexts; and (3) Congress' enactment of Title VII was an exercise of its powers under Section 5. The decision was unanimous. Justice Rehnquist wrote the majority opinion; Justices Brennan and Stevens wrote concurring opinions. (Fitzpatrick v. Bitzer, US SupCt-1976, 12 FEP Cases 1586)	This case took on added significance because of a decision handed down four days earlier holding unconstitutional the 1974 amendments to the Fair Labor Standards Act that extended minimum-wage and overtime-pay protection to almost all nonsupervisory employees of state and local governments (National League of Cities v. Usery, US SupCt-1976, 22 WH Cases 1064) For a discussion of the Equal Pay Act, see below under "Equal Pay Act; Constitutionality: Public Sector."
Damages: Compensatory, Punitive—Act of 1866 Action	An individual who establishes a cause of action under the Civil Rights Act of 1866 (42 U.S.C. Sec. 1981) is entitled to both equitable and legal relief including compensatory and, under certain circumstances, punitive damages. Remedies available under Section 1981 and those available under Title VII of Civil Rights Act of 1964, although related and directed to most of same ends, are separate, distinct, and independent. (Johnson v. Railway Express Agency, US SupCt-1975, 10 FEP Cases 817)	The case involved another issue of the tolling of the state statute of limitations applicable to action. For a discussion of the holding on this issue, see below under "Tolling of Action under the 1866 Act."

Issue	Holding	Comment
Civil Rights Act, Title VII: Procedures—Contd. Damages: Compensatory, Punitive—Title VII action	In a strong opinion, the Sixth Circuit reversed a district court decision awarding a group of employees back pay for three years, applying a state statute of limitations, plus $4,000,000 in punitive damages against the employer, Detroit Edison Co., and $250,000 against Local 223 of the Utility Workers. In reversing the judgment, the appeals court pointed out that damages are a legal not an equitable remedy, and the Seventh Amendment to the U.S. Constitution requires a jury trial in an action under a statute that creates legal rights and remedies. But a demand for a jury trial by the employer and the union was rejected. Moreover, the court added, the "other equitable relief as the court deems appropriate" specified in Section 706(g) of Title VII is limited to relief in the form of restitution. The court also ruled that an individual who sues both under Title VII and 42 U.S.C. Sec. 1981 (1866 Act) does not enlarge his right to relief beyond that authorized by Title VII. Section 1981 contains no provision for relief by way of damages, and when it is joined with another statutory right of action, such as Title VII, which specifies broad equitable remedies, there is no enlarging those remedies to include legal relief by punitive damages. (EEOC v. Detroit Edison Co., Local 17 of EBEW and Local 223 of Utility Workers; Stamps v. same, CA 6-1975, 10 FEP Cases 239) The case was taken to the Supreme Court, which vacated the judgment and remanded the case to the Sixth Circuit for further consideration in light of the decision in Teamsters v. U.S., 14 FEP Cases 1514.(Local 223, Utility Workers, et al. v. EEOC, US SupCt-1977, 14 FEP Cases 1686) The case later was settled.	The remand in the Detroit Edison case left some questions unanswered concerning the relationship of Title VII to Section 1981 regarding the award of compensatory and punitive damages. Johnson v. Railway Express Agency, supra, established the right to recover such damages under Section 1981. But Detroit Edison appeared to rule them out under Title VII. What about a combined action under both Title VII and Section 1981? This was the situation in Detroit Edison. Since the remand, there have been some circuit court decisions upholding the award of damages in combined Title VII - Section 1981 actions. These are discussed below.
Damages: Punitive—Combined Title VII, 1866 Act Action Title VII—Section 1981 Action	An employer properly was assessed punitive damages for its violations of the Civil Rights Act of 1866, the Fifth Circuit ruled, even though it was sued not only under the 1866 Act (42 U.S.C. Sec. 1981) but also under Title VII, which has been held not to authorize an award of punitive damages. The appeals court found the trial court's award of punitive damages does not so conflict with the purpose embodied in Title VII that it should be disallowed in a combined action. (Claiborne v. Illinois Central RR, CA 5-1978, 18 FEP Cases 536) A similar ruling was handed down by the Eighth Circuit in affirming an award of $1,000 punitive dam-	The appeals court also approved the amount—$50,000—that the district court awarded. It explained that the employer's intransigence in failing before the suit was filed to redress genuinely any of its prior discriminatory acts, plus its additional acts of post-Act discrimination, such as testing only black helpers to evaluate their asserted "deficiencies," supported the trial court's view that the employer acted with malice toward its black employees.

Issue	Holding	Comment
Civil Rights Act, Title VII: Procedures—Contd. Damages: Punitive—Combined Title VII, 1866 Act Action Title VII—Section 1981 Action—Contd.	ages against the defendants in an action joining Section 1981 and Title VII claims. (Allen v. Amalgamated Transit Union, Local 788, CA 8-1977, 14 FEP Cases 1494, cert. denied, US SupCt-1977, 15 FEP Cases 1184) See also Bradshaw v. Zoological Society of San Diego, CA 9-1978, 16 FEP Cases 828, in which the court stated that general and punitive damages are not barred where Section 1983(Civil Rights Act of 1871) and Title VII claims have been joined.	
Disclosure of Information: Affidavits of Charging Parties	In a case involving the disclosure of affidavits filed by employees and former employees in support of Title VII charges against an employer, the Fourth Circuit made these rulings: ● The exemption under the Freedom of Information Act (FOIA) for matters specifically exempted from disclosure by statute does not apply to affidavits filed with the EEOC by charging parties in support of a charge against an employer, notwithstanding the provisions of Title VII forbidding the EEOC to make public charges filed with it, and making it unlawful for an EEOC office or employee to make public, prior to the institution of any proceeding, any information obtained by the EEOC. ● Affidavits of former employees were not exempt from disclosure under the exemption in the FOIA for investigatory records whose disclosure would interfere with enforcement proceedings. ● Affidavits of present employees were exempt from disclosure under exemption in the FOIA for investigatory records whose disclosure would interfere with enforcement proceedings. (Charlotte-Mecklenburg Hospital Authority v. Perry, CA 4-1978, 16 FEP Cases 680)	The Supreme Court has held that information submitted to the government by a government contractor pursuant to Executive Order 11246 is not exempt from disclosure under the FOIA. For a discussion of this holding see above under "Executive Order 11246: Disclosure of Information." Also, the NLRB has held that a union bargaining agent that has a nondiscrimination clause in its contract is entitled to information concerning the employer's EEOC practices. (See Westinghouse Electric Corp., NLRB-1978, 99 LRRM 1482)

Issue	Holding	Comment
Civil Rights Act, Title VII: Procedures—Contd. Filing of Charge: Expansion of Case	EEOC may sue a respondent under Title VII for any discrimination stated in the charge or developed in the course of a reasonable investigation of the charge, so long as such discrimination is included within the reasonable cause determination and the conciliation process. So the EEOC was held to have the right to sue an employer for alleged sex discrimination in promotion and transfer in addition to alleged racial discrimination, even though charges filed with the EEOC alleged only racial discrimination, since facts on which the EEOC based its responsible cause finding of sex discrimination were developed in the course of investigation of charges. (EEOC v. General Electric Co., CA 4-1976, 12 FEP Cases 21)	One charge, the court pointed out, referred particularly to certain tests required of all job applicants, and these tests, which were produced by the company voluntarily, constituted evidence by the EEOC as authorizing its findings of reasonable cause to believe there was racial and sex discrimination. The claims of racial and sex discrimination are "like" or "related" in that they involve the same tests. In support of its holding, the court cited, among others, Sanchez v. Standard Brands, CA 5-1970, 2 FEP Cases 788.
Filing of Charge: Oath or Affirmation—Commissioner's Charge	A charge filed by an EEOC Commissioner that was not made under oath or affirmation, as required by Section 706(b) of Title VII, is not a valid charge, since the requirements of Section 706(b) are mandatory. The trial court correctly held that it lacked jurisidiction over the EEOC's subsequent Title VII action because the invalid charge did not give the EEOC jurisdiction to proceed with the investigation. (EEOC v. Appalachian Power Co., CA 4-1978, 16 FEP Cases 390)	The Commissioner later filed an affidavit stating that his failure to swear to the charge was inadvertent. The district court pointed out that the affidavit was improperly notarized. The district court also noted that when the Commision made its reasonable cause determination, it specifically rejected two of the Commissioner's allegations. This casts doubt, the court said, on whether the Commissioner had sufficient information regarding his allegations before him at the time he was required to swear that his allegations were true. (EEOC v. Appalachian Power Co., USDC WVa-1976, 13 FEP Cases 1294)
Filing of Charge: Oath or Affirmation—Private Party's Charge	A federal district court's jurisdiction of an action by a female applicant for employment alleging sex discrimination under Title VII did not depend on whether the charge of discrimination filed with the EEOC was under oath. The statutory provisions for verification of the charge relates solely to administrative rather than judicial features of the Act, and the provision is directory and technical, rather than mandatory and substantive. (Choate v. Caterpillar Tractor Co., CA 7-1968, 1 FEP Cases 431) The case involved another issue involving the requirement of conciliation efforts by the EEOC. The decision on this issue is discussed above under "Concilation by EEOC."	Although this case involved a charge filed by a private party, while Appalachian Power discussed above involved a Commissioner's charge, there would appear to be some conflict in the reasoning.

Issue	Holding	Comment
Civil Rights Act, Title VII: Procedures—Contd. Filing of Charge: Title VII—State Filing	Where a state has a law prohibiting an unlawful employment practice, no charge may be filed with the EEOC before 60 days after proceedings have been commenced in the appropriate state agency, unless such proceedings have been terminated earlier. Moreover, Section 706(e) requires that a charge be filed in such a state within 300 days after the alleged violation occurred or within 30 days after the aggrieved person receives notice that the state agency has terminated the proceedings. So that the former employee's charge in this case, filed 351 days after the alleged violation occurred was not timely filed. The decision was by a six-to-three margin, with Justices Blackmun, Brennan, and Marshall dissenting. (Mohasco Corp v. Silver, US SupCt-1980, 23 FEP Cases 1)	The plaintiff filed a letter with the EEOC 291 days after he was discharged, alleging that he was discriminated against because of his religion. Then more than 60 days after receiving the letter and 351 days after the discharge, the EEOC notified the employer that a charge had been filed against it. A year later, the EEOC issued a determination that there was no reasonable cause to believe the charge was true and notified the plaintiff that he had a statutory right to file a private action. He filed an action 91 days later. In holding that the action was not timely filed, the court said that Congress clearly intended to encourage the prompt processing of all employment discrimination charges.
Filing of Charge: Title VII, 1866 Act	In a case drawing on earlier civil rights legislation, the U.S. Court of Appeals at Chicago held that a black former employee and a black job applicant could maintain an action against a union for allegedly assisting in the maintenance of a racially discriminatory hiring system, even though the aggrieved persons did not file a charge against the union with the EEOC. The action could be maintained under the Civil Rights Act of 1866, as amended, the court said. (Waters v. Wisconsin Steel Works and the United Order of American Bricklayers and Stone Masons, Local 21, CA 7-1970, 2 FEP Cases 574) The Supreme Court later denied review of the case. (Wisconsin Steel Works of International Harvester Co. v. Waters, US SupCt-1970, 2 FEP Cases 1059) In a later case, the U.S. Court of Appeals for the Third Circuit also held that a victim of alleged racial discrimination in employment may go directly into court under the 1866 Act—now Section 1981 of Title 42 of the U.S. Code. The plaintiff, the court said, would not have to await completion of the deferral and conciliation procedures under Title VII. (Young v. International Telephone & Telegraph Co., CA 3-1971, 3 FEP Cases 146)	Under the 1964 Act, a charge could be filed under oath by a person aggrieved or by a member of the Commission. The EEOC took the position that this provision precluded organizations, such as unions or civil rights groups, from filing charges on behalf of victims of alleged discrimination. But under the 1972 amendments, a charge also may be filed "or on behalf of" a person allegedly aggrieved. This permits aggrieved persons to have charges processed in situations in which they are unwilling to come forward publicly for fear of reprisal.
Finding of Reasonable Cause	In a decision handed down in 1973, the Supreme Court held that the absence of a finding by the EEOC of "reasonable cause" to believe a violation had occurred does not bar a suit by an aggrieved individual. He satisfies the jurisdic-	Prior to the Supreme Court decision, the lower courts had divided on the issue of a finding of "reasonable cause." But in one major decision by the U.S. Court of Appeals for the Third Circuit, the court reached the same conclusion

Issue	Holding	Comment
Civil Rights Act, Title VII: Procedures—Contd. Finding of Reasonable Cause—Contd.	tional requirements, the Court said, by filing timely charges with the EEOC and by receiving and acting upon the EEOC's statutory notice of the right to sue. Title VII does not restrict an individual's right to sue to those charges on which the EEOC has made findings of "reasonable cause." (McDonnell Douglas Corp. v. Green, US SupCt-1973, 5 FEP Cases 965)	later reached by the Supreme Court in the McDonnell Douglas case. The appeals court said: "Good reason and fealty to the spirit and purpose of the Act command that we do not require an affirmative finding by the Commission as a passport for judicial review." (Fekete v. U.S. Steel Corp., CA 3-1970, 2 FEP Cases 540)
Intervention by EEOC	In cases decided prior to the 1972 amendments, two courts of appeals—those for the Fifth and Seventh Circuits—held that the EEOC may not intervene as a matter of right in an action brought under Title VII. They also held that the EEOC does not have standing to challenge as insufficient a settlement agreement between representatives of a class and an employer. (Braddy v. Southern Bell T&T Co., CA 5-1972, 4 FEP Cases 174; Stewards v. American Airlines, Inc., CA 7-1972, 4 FEP Cases 152) The U.S. Court of Appeals for the Sixth Circuit, meanwhile, held that a federal district court did not abuse its discretion in denying a motion by the EEOC for permissive intervention in a Title VII action. (Thornton v. East Texas Motor Freight, CA 6-1972, 4 FEP Cases 205)	Under the 1972 amendments, the EEOC was given power to file an action in a federal district court upon a finding of reasonable cause to believe a violation of Title VII has been committed. So the right to intervene in private suits has become less important.
		Since the 1972 amendments, there have been decisions by three circuit courts of appeals dealing with the right of intervention with differing results. The holdings were as follows: ● Where the EEOC has failed to obtain conciliation of the charge, notifies the aggrieved individual of the right to sue, and the aggrieved individual sues within the required statutory period, the EEOC may not later bring a separate suit based on the same charge. There is only a right of intervention. The aggrieved individual has an absolute right to intervene if the EEOC has filed a suit. The EEOC has a permissive right to intervene if the charging party has brought an action. (EEOC v. Missouri Pacific RR Co., CA 8-1974, 7 FEP Cases 177) ● The EEOC apparently is restricted to an intervenor's status once a private action has been filed. (EEOC v. Occidental Life Insurance Co., CA 9-1976, 12 FEP Cases 1300) This case later was reviewed by the Supreme Court on a "statute of limitations" issue.

Issue	Holding	Comment
Civil Rights Act, Title VII: Procedures—Contd. Intervention by EEOC—Contd.		● The EEOC has the power under the 1972 amendments to bring a suit, and it does not lose that power when a private party brings a suit based on the same facts. (EEOC v. North Hills Passavant Hospital, CA 3-1976, 13 FEP Cases 1129)
Limiting of Actions: Continuing Violation	Charges were timely filed by a group of laid-off female employees, even though the layoffs occurred more than 90 days (now 180 days) before the charges were filed, since the charges alleged that the alleged layoffs were "continuing." (Cox v. U.S. Gypsum, CA 7-1969, 70 LRRM 3278, 1 FEP Cases 714)	The court also noted that the recent hiring of new employees suggested discriminatory recalls.
	A female former flight attendant who failed to file a timely charge challenging her 1968 separation from employment pursuant to the airline's "no-marriage" rule and who was rehired in 1972 as a new employee may not challenge the airline's failure to credit her with her pre-1972 seniority, notwithstanding her claim that the charge she filed in 1973 was timely because the airline is guilty of a "present, continuing violation" of Title VII. She failed to allege that the airline's seniority system, which is neutral in its operation, discriminates against female former employee or treats discriminatorily discharged employees any differently than former employees who resigned or were discharged for nondiscriminatory reasons. It was a seven-to-two decision, with Justices Marshall and Brennan dissenting. (United Air Lines v. Evans, US SupCt-1977, 14 FEP Cases 1510)	Prior to the Evans case, the law of continuing violations had been both complicated and confusing. This was partly because there are a number of different theories under which the courts had found such violations to exist and partly because the facts involved and the concepts applied made it difficult to draw clear-cut lines of distinction. Many of the cases involved airlines and the rule involved in Evans requiring stewardesses to resign or be terminated upon being married.
Limiting of Actions: Delay of EEOC	The period for which an unlawfully rejected job applicant may recover back pay under Title VII may be reduced by the period of time—more than four years—that her charge remained at the EEOC following the expiration of the first 180 days after the charge was filed. Under the EEOC's regulations, the employee automatically could have obtained a notice of right to sue merely by requesting one any time following the expiration of 180 days after the charge was filed. (Kamberos v. GTE Automatic Electric, Inc., CA 7-1979, 20 FEP Cases 602)	The court refused, however, to reduce the back pay period because of the delay in the courts. The case was assigned to three different judges before it was heard by a fourth judge more than three years after the action was brought.

Issue	Holding	Comment
Civil Rights Act, Title VII: Procedures—Contd. Limiting of Actions: Delay of State Agency	A state agency's six-year delay in processing a complaint filed under Title VII does not toll the time limit for pressing the charge with the EEOC. Title VII requires the filing of charges with the EEOC within 180 days after the alleged violations, within 300 days of the alleged violation if charges are filed with a state agency, or within 30 days after learning that the state completed proceedings on the complaint, if the state takes final action before the 30-day limit expires. Although the court found the state agency's delay "inexcusable," it could find no ground to toll Title VII's time bar. The language permitting filing with the EEOC within 30 days after the state agency has finished proceedings in a case "only operates to cut short the 300-day period," the court said, "it cannot lengthen it." (Daughtry v. King's Department Stores, Inc., CA 1-1979, 21 FEP Cases 333)	The court noted decisions in other cases have permitted "equitable tolling" of Title VII's time limit. But in those cases, it said, the late filing resulted from misleading action by the employer or the state agency. In this case, there was no evidence that the late filing wth the EEOC was caused by the state or federal agency or by the employer.
Limiting of Actions: EEOC Action	The EEOC is not required by Section 706(f)(1) of Title VII to bring an action in court within 180 days of the filing of a charge. Section 706(f)(1) simply provides that the charging party whose charge is not dismissed, promptly settled, or litigated by the EEOC must wait 180 days before bringing his own action. The concern of Congress for need of time limitations in the fair operation of Title VII, as reflected in the 1972 amendments, was directed entirely to the initial filing of the charge with the EEOC and with prompt notification of the filing to the charged party; the statute of limitations problem was not perceived in terms of a limitation on the EEOC's power to sue. Moreover, Title VII actions brought by the EEOC are not subject to state statutes of limitations. Justice Stewart wrote the opinion of the Court. Chief Justice Burger and Justice Rehnquist dissented. (Occidental Life Ins. Co. v. EEOC, US SupCt-1977, 14 FEP Cases 1718)	The result of the holding was that the EEOC was permitted to maintain an action that it brought approximately three years and two months after the charge was filed with it and five months after conciliation efforts had failed, even though the analogous state limitations period was one year.
Limiting of Actions: 1866 Civil Rights Act	Colorado's six-year statute of limitations applicable to tort and contract actions governs an action brought by an employee under the Civil Rights Act of 1866 alleging employment discrimination on the basis of national origin. The court pointed out that the U.S. Supreme Court had held that since the 1866 Act does not contain a statute of limitations, it is federal policy to apply the most appropriate one pro-	The Civil Rights Act of 1866 provides that "all persons ... shall have the same right ... to make and enforce contracts ... as is enjoyed by white citizens." This language, the court stated, indicates the contractual nature of an action under the Act. While recognizing that claims of employment discrimination may be founded on interference with the personal right to contract and so can be said to sound in tort,

Issue	Holding	Comment
Civil Rights Act, Title VII: Procedures—Contd. Limiting of Actions: 1866 Civil Rights Act—Contd.	vided by the state law. (Johnson v. Railway Express Agency, US SupCt-1975, 10 FEP Cases 817; Auto Workers v. Hoosier Corp., US SupCt-1966, 61 LRRM 2545; Runyon v. McCrary, US SupCt-1976, 427 US 160) The court noted that under Colorado law there is a statute of limitations governing federal actions that sets a two-year period. But if a comparable state action sets a longer period, that longer period controls. The court concluded that the facts in an employment discrimination case under the 1866 Act will most closely resemble those in either a contract or tort claim. So it decided that the six-year statute of limitations for tort and contract actions applies to an action under the 1866 Act. (Zuniga v. Amfac Foods, CA 10-1978, 17 FEP Cases 1195)	the court observed, the same time limitation applies to both tort and contract claims. But see Davis v. U.S. Steel Supply, CA 3-1978, 17 FEP Cases 1190, in which the court refused to apply a state personal injury statute of limitations to an action under Section 1981.
Limiting of Actions: Equitable Tolling	Failure of a former employee to file a timely charge with the EEOC should not serve, under all circumstances, to bar the maintenance of an action under Title VII. To effectuate the broad remedial purposes of the statute, the time limitations should be subject to a similar type of equitable tolling as is applied to statutes of limitations. In finding that the period for filing an EEO charge is not jurisdictional in nature, the Third Circuit noted that the statutory procedures are initiated by laymen unfamiliar with the complexities of the administrative process. (Hart v. J.T. Baker Chemical Co., CA 3-1979, 19 FEP Cases 1347)	In the particular case, the court ruled that the doctrine of equitable tolling was not available to a former employee who claimed she filed her charge late because she did not discover until five months after her discharge that she may have been discriminated against. The court said that her suspicions at the time of her discharge were sufficient to lead a reasonable person to inquire further into the reasons for discharge.
	Time limitations for filing a charge under Title VII are jurisdictional in the sense that the phrase is used in relation to statutes of limitations, and equitable principles should apply in circumstances which warrant their application. So reasoning, the Sixth Circuit held that equitable grounds in a case involving the University of Cincinnati tolled the running of the 180-day period for filing a charge with the EEOC. Within the 180-day period, the plaintiff employee learned that the University had filled a position that she had sought. Her attorney consulted with the University's attorney who wrote that it had been agreed that he would be given sufficient time to research the matter in return for any assurance that time for this investigation "will not be used by the University in any way to prejudice your client's rights with	The Sixth Circuit noted that the Supreme Court has not expressly addressed the issue whether Title VII time periods may be tolled on equitable grounds. But in a case decided in 1972, the Sixth Circuit itself had clearly held that in appropriate circumstances, Title VII time periods may be tolled on equitable grounds. (Harris v. Walgreen's Distributing Center, CA 6-1972, 4 FEP Cases 342) In a later case, a three-judge panel of the Fifth Circuit divided three ways on the issue of "equitable modification" of the 180-day limitation on the filing of a charge under Title VII. Two judges held that there should be some equitable modification of the time limit, but only one would modify it under the circumstances of the case. The employee had relied on the representations of a Texas Employment

Issue	Holding	Comment
Civil Rights Act, Title VII: Procedures—Contd. Limiting of Actions: Equitable Tolling—Contd.	regard to any statute of limitations." The University rejected the employee's claim of discrimination some six weeks later, and the employee filed a charge with the EEOC, but more than 180 days after her claim arose. In ruling for the employee, the Sixth Circuit observed that the correspondence clearly put the University on notice that the employee was asserting her rights pursuant to Title VII and provided the University with the protections that limitation periods are intended to provide. The University's express statements that it would not use the time spent in its investigation to prejudice the employee, and the employee's reliance on these statements, reasonably could have led her to delay filing a charge with the EEOC. It reversed the lower court's dismissal of the action. (Leake v. University of Cincinnati, CA 6-1979, 20 FEP Cases 964)	Commission employee that her complaint had been forwarded to the EEOC. The third judge took the position that the limitation period is a jurisdictional requirement to which "equitable considerations should be irrelevant." (Chappell v. Emco Machine Works Co., CA 5-1979, 20 FEP Cases 1059) Earlier, a three-judge panel of the same court, with only one member the same, had held unanimously that the 90-day filing requirement was not "jurisdictional" in the sense that compliance with the requirement determines the jurisdiction of the court without respect to any other circumstances in the particular case. The requirement, the court said, should be analogized to a statute of limitations, thus permitting application of equitable modifications, such as tolling and estoppel. (Reeb v. Economic Opportunity of Atlanta, CA 5-1975, 11 FEP Cases 235) But see an Eighth Circuit holding that the 90-day filing period is a jurisdictional requirement for bringing an action that may not be waived. (Hinton v. CPC International, Inc., CA 8-1975, 10 FEP Cases 1423) Also see an Eighth Circuit holding that the 180-day period was not tolled while a former railroad employee pursued a remedy before the National Railroad Adjustment Board. (Harris v. Norfolk & Western Ry. Co., CA 8-1980, 22 FEP Cases 472)
Limiting of Actions: Filing of Grievance	In another case involving a university, the Supreme Court held by a five-to-four margin that the time for filing a charge challenging a university's denial of tenure to a professor may not be extended for the one-year grace period given the professor to find another job. The time limit began, the Court said, the day the university informed the professor he would be offered a one-year terminal contract. (Delaware State College v. Ricks, US SupCt-1980, 24 FEP Cases 827)	
Limiting of Actions: Futility of Charge	An employer and racially separate unions were not entitled to summary judgment in an action under Title VII by an injured black longshoreman, although a federal district court had granted such judgment. The district court had held that the longshoreman was not a person aggrieved under Title VII because he had not	In a footnote, the appeals court questioned whether the 90-day requirement is a jurisdictional prerequisite to a Title VII action. The 90-day requirement seems to be directed toward ensuring that the EEOC expend its conciliation resources only on alleged unlawful employment practices that are reasonably current.

Issue	Holding	Comment
Civil Rights Act, Title VII: Procedures—Contd. Limiting of Actions: Futility of Charge—Contd.	filed his charge with the EEOC within 90 days (now 180 days) of the last time he applied for work. The appellate court noted that the longshoreman testified that he was physically capable of performing only certain jobs that were reserved exclusively for white workers, and that it would have been futile to have applied for these jobs within the 90-day period. Such testimony created disputed issues of material fact, the appeals court stated. (Boudreaux v. Baton Rouge Marine Co., CA 5-1971, 3 FEP Cases 99)	
		The 1972 amendments to Title VII raised the 90-day time limit for filing a charge to 180 days. Moreover, if a charge initially is filed with a state or local agency within 180 days after the alleged unlawful practice occurred, a charge must be filed with the EEOC within 300 days after the alleged practice occurred, or within 30 days after receiving notice that the state or local agency has terminated its proceedings, whichever occurs first.
Notice of Charge: Delay in Serving	An employer that did not receive a notice from the EEOC of the filing of a charge within 10 days, as required by Section 706(b) of Title VII, did not show a denial of due process sufficient to bar the EEOC from suing, where the EEOC made every attempt to comply with the conditions precedent to a suit, including the mailing of notice to the employer within the 10-day period, and where there was no clear showing of substantial prejudice to the employer resulting from its delay in receiving the notice. The case was remanded for a determination of the extent of prejudice, if any, that the employer suffered because of the lack of receipt of a timely notice. Even if substantial prejudice should be found to have occurred, the court added, it would not necessarily defeat the entire case but only the portion of it affected by that prejudice. (EEOC v. Airguide Corp., CA 5-1976, 13 FEP Cases 904)	In a case decided four years earlier, the Fifth Circuit held that a district court improperly set aside a demand by the EEOC for access to evidence against an employer that was not served with the charge filed by an aggrieved employee for more than a year after the charge was filed with the EEOC. The district court found that the EEOC had not served the employer with a notice of charge within a reasonable time. But the appeals court said that, even assuming that the Administrative Procedure Act creates mandatory duties on administrative agencies sufficient to set aside agency action as unlawful if unreasonably delayed, the employer made no showing that it had been prejudiced. (Chromcraft Corp. v. EEOC, CA 5-1972, 4 FEP Cases 1085)
Pattern–or–Practice Actions: Private Sector	In an action by the U.S. Attorney General under Section 707 of the Civil Rights Act of 1964, the establishment of an unrestricted plant-wide seniority and bidding plan was held not approporiate, notwithstanding the contention	In another pattern or practice case involving a union, the court entered judgment for the Attorney General. It found that the evidence, including that relating to discrimination by the union prior to the effective date of the Act,

Issue	Holding	Comment
Civil Rights Act, Title VII: Procedures—Contd. Pattern-or-Practice Actions: Private Sector—Contd.	that such a plan was needed to compensate black employees for past discrimination and to achieve a more proportionate racial balance. Under the facts and the legislative history of the Act, the court said, the proposed remedy was not justified. There were substantial opportunities for upward and horizontal mobility, there were significant differences between the departments to which bidding presently is limited, and the employees whom the Attorney General intended to benefit often had declined available progression opportunities in the past. (U.S. v. H.K. Porter Co., USDC NAla-1968, 70 LRRM 2131, 1 FEP Cases 515)	justified an order in favor of the Attorney General. But the court did not require the union, which was all-white as a result of pre-Act discrimination against blacks to take affirmative action to relieve the present-day result of pre-Act discrimination, since that would constitute the granting of unlawful preferential treatment to blacks. (Dobbins v. Local 212, IBEW, USDC SOhio-1968, 69 LRRM 2313, 1 FEP Cases 387) (For a broad order in a pattern-or-practice case, see U.S. v. Medical Society of South Carolina, USDC SC-1969, 71 LRRM 2057, 1 FEP Cases 725.)
	A federal district court erred in denying a preliminary injunction sought by the Attorney General in a pattern-or-practice action brought against an employer charged with racial discrimination in hiring, transfer, and promotion. The lower court answered the wrong question in deciding the issue, according to the appeals court. Shortly after the action was filed, the company was awarded a government contract that resulted in a substantial increase in its work force. So the company and the union negotiated a new agreement that loosened transfer procedures somewhat in favor of black employees. The lower court denied the injunction largely because it concluded that the new transfer program did not violate Title VII. But the appeals court said that the question was whether the fact that the new union contract and the transfer program partially corrected violations shown by the Attorney General negated the need for the injunction. It decided that it did not, finding that the Attorney General should prevail on the merits. (U.S. v. Hayes International Corp., CA 5-1969, 2 FEP Cases 67)	In holding that the injunction should have been issued, the appeals court said: "We take the position that in such a case, irreparable injury should be presumed from the very fact that the statute has been violated. Whenever a qualified Negro employee is discriminatorily denied a chance to fill a position for which he is qualified and has the seniority to obtain, he suffers irreparable injury and so does the labor force of the country as a whole." In a case involving joint apprenticeship and training committees in the Seattle area, the U.S. Court of Appeals for the Tenth Circuit concluded that "it was the intent of Congress that a 'pattern or practice' should be found where the acts of discrimination are not 'isolated, peculiar, or accidental events.' " It rejected a lower court ruling that the term "pattern or practice" should be interpreted as meaning "uniformly engaged in a course of conduct aimed at denying rights secured by the Act." (U.S. v. Ironworkers Local 86, CA 9-1971, 3 FEP Cases 496, cert. denied, US SupCt-1971, 4 FEP Cases 37)
	Finding pattern and practice of discrimination against blacks in violation of Title VII, the U.S. Court of Appeals at St. Louis fashioned a broad order designed to eliminate the past violations. The court ordered the local unions involved to modify referral systems to permit blacks who are reasonably qualified to register for employment at the locals' hiring halls and to be placed in the highest groups for which they qualify. They also were ordered to modify experience requirements for blacks otherwise qualified and to take reasonable steps to publicize to the black community that all persons now are	In its decision, the appeals court reversed a federal district court holding and rejected a contention that the government is required to prove specific instances of discrimination after the effective date of the Act.

Issue	Holding	Comment
Civil Rights Act, Title VII: Procedures—Contd. Pattern-or-Practice Actions: Private Sector—Contd.	permitted to use the referrel system. One local also was ordered to modify its journeyman's examination procedure so that the examination is objective in nature, is designed to test the ability of the applicant to perform journeyman's work, and is given and graded in such a manner as to permit review. (U.S. v. Sheet Metal Workers, CA 8-1969, 2 FEP Cases 127)	
Pattern-or-Practice Actions: Public Sector	The U.S. Attorney General has the authority to bring a pattern-or-practice action under Title VII against a public employer, such as a school district, without having the matter referred to him from the EEOC. In so ruling, the Ninth Circuit relied in part on the President's Reorganization Plan of 1978 that transferred authority to initiate pattern-or-practice actions in the public sector from the EEOC to the Attorney General. It suggested, moreover, that the Attorney General had this authority even before the Reorganization Plan became effective. (U.S. v. Fresno School District, CA 9-1979, 19 FEP Cases 408)	The Fourth Circuit handed down a similar holding in reversing a lower court holding that the Attorney General lacked authority to bring public-sector pattern-or-practice actions in view of the 1972 amendments to Title VII transferring authority to bring pattern-or-practice actions from the Attorney General to the EEOC. (U.S. v. State of North Carolina, CA 4-1978, 19 FEP Cases 407) In the Fresno case, the Ninth Circuit noted that a number of federal district courts and the Sixth Circuit had held that the Attorney General did not have independent authority to bring a pattern-or-practice action against a public employer without a referral from the EEOC. (U.S. v. Board of Education, Garfield Heights, CA 6-1978, 19 FEP Cases 406) But the Ninth Circuit pointed out that the 1972 amendments provided that public sector Title VII actions would be brought by the Attorney General. It added that the legislative history surrounding the 1978 Reorganization Plan indicated that the district courts and the Sixth Circuit were wrong in holding that the Attorney General could not initiate public sector pattern-or-practice actions.
Prior Resort to State Agency	An Arizona black job applicant's action under Title VII of the Act was ordered dismissed by the Ninth Circuit because the applicant filed a charge directly with the EEOC without first going to the Arizona Civil Rights Commission. The applicant had relied upon advice by the EEOC's General Counsel that the Arizona Commission lacked authority "to grant or seek relief" within the meaning of Section 706(b) of the Act, since it could not enforce a cease-and-desist order unless a respondent already had been served with cease-and desist order involving a prior violation. The court disagreed, stating that the "relief" mentioned in the Act refers to what the state agency may seek and	The Arizona Commission not only seeks relief in precisely the same fashion as the EEOC does, the appeals court observed, but it seeks precisely the same relief as well as the elimination of the unlawful practice by "conference, conciliation, and persuasion." The Supreme Court did not disturb the finding as to the status of the Arizona Commission, although dissenting Justice Douglas would have granted review on the point. It remanded the case to the district court for consideration of the position advanced by the Solicitor General that the court should retain jurisdiction for a period sufficient to allow the individual bringing the charge to go before the State Commis-

Issue	Holding	Comment
Civil Rights Act, Title VII: Procedures—Contd. Prior Resort to State Agency—Contd.	not to what the state courts may grant. (Crosslin v. Mountain States T. & T. Co., CA 9-1970, 2 FEP Cases 480) The Supreme Court later vacated the order of the appeals court dismissing the action and remanded the case. (Crosslin v. Mountain States Telephone Co., US SupCt-1971, 3 FEP Cases 70)	sion. It added that it was expressing no opinion as to the merits of the Solicitor General's position.
	A person claiming to be aggrieved may maintain an action under Title VII of the Civil Rights Act of 1964, the U.S. Supreme Court ruled, even though he did not follow strictly the procedure outlined in the Act for filing a charge with the EEOC. Section 706(b) provides that where there is a state or local agency authorized to deal with employment discrimination, no charge may be filed with the EEOC before the expiration of 60 days after proceedings have been commenced under the state or local law, unless such proceedings have been terminated earlier. Section 706(d) requires the charge to be filed within 30 days after receipt of notice that the state or local agency has terminated its proceedings. In this case, the plaintiff filed directly with the EEOC, which referred the charge to the Colorado Commission. After the Colorado Commission terminated its jurisdiction, the EEOC formally filed the charge without obtaining a new charge from the aggrieved individual. The Supreme Court said that the procedure followed by the EEOC complied with the purpose behind both sections of the Act. (Love v. Pullman Co., US Sup Ct-1972, 4 FEP Cases 150)	The Supreme Court reversed a decision by the U.S. Court of Appeals for the Tenth Circuit. (Love v. Pullman Co., CA 10-1969, 2 FEP Cases 141) In seeking review, the EEOC contended that the decision of the appeals court would affect more than 25 percent of the charges filed with it each year.
Prior Suit by Charging Party	The filing of an action under Title VII of the Civil Rights Act of 1964 by a charging party bars the EEOC from later filing its own action based on the same charge. The EEOC action was based on the 1972 amendments giving it power to sue. The U.S. Court of Appeals for the Eighth Circuit handed down this ruling in affirming a district court's dismissal of the EEOC's action. The charging party alleged that the company discriminated against him because of his race and religious creed when it refused to hire him under its policy of not hiring persons convicted of a criminal offense other than a minor traffic violation. He had been convicted of failure to report for military induction. The appeals court, however, agreed with the lower	At least two district courts have taken the same position as the appeals court that prior filing by a charging party bars a suit by the EEOC. (EEOC v. Union Oil Co. of Calif., USDC NAla-1974, 6 FEP Cases 1298; EEOC v. McLean Trucking Co., USDC WTenn-1974) Several courts also have held that the EEOC must comply with its own regulations in filing an action. See above under "Conciliation by EEOC" for cases on this issue.

Issue	Holding	Comment
Civil Rights Act, Title VII: Procedures—Contd. Prior Suit by Charging Party—Contd.	court's ruling that the EEOC may intervene in the charging party's action. In addition, it suggested that the district court consider the EEOC's plea to expand the action to cover the issues it sought to raise in its own action. The court took note of Section 706(f) of the Act. Once either the EEOC or the charging party files an action, the court observed, the statute speaks only in terms of intervention. (EEOC v. Missouri Pacific R.R. Co., CA 8-1974, 7 FEP Cases 177) For discussion of other aspects of the case see "Class Actions" above and "Substantive Rulings: Arrest and Conviction Record: Use in Hiring" below.	
Res judicata, Collateral Estoppel: Prior State Proceedings	Doctrines of res judicata and collateral estoppel do not bar an employee who prevailed at a state administrative level from bringing a Title VII action after the employer appealed to a state trial court and lost and then appealed to a state appellate court, which reversed the trial court and dismissed the employee's complaint. Title VII creates a special circumstance that warrants an exception to the normal rules of collateral estoppel. The prior state proceedings, however, are entitled to weight in factual determinations of a federal court that is considering the Title VII action. (Gunther v. Iowa State Men's Reformatory, CA 8-1980, 21 FEP Cases 1031)	The court noted a Second Circuit decision holding that, if a state court has passed on an FEP claim, the complainant may not thereafter bring action on the same claim under Title VII. (Sinicropi v. Nassau County, see below.) But the Eighth Circuit stated that until the Sinicropi holding, the federal courts deciding Title VII claims consistently had refused to give res judicata and collateral estoppel effect to state discrimination claims decided by state courts.
	If a state court has passed on an FEP claim, the complainant may not thereafter bring an action under Title VII in a federal court. The Second Circuit applied the doctrine of res judicata to a woman who brought a Title VII action after her claims of sex discrimination by an employer and improper processing of her complaint by a state FEP Agency were rejected in state administrative and judicial proceedings. The court pointed out that in Mitchell v. National Broadcasting Co. (CA 2-1977, 14 FEP Cases 1034), it ruled that an individual whose discrimination claim was rejected by a state court could not subsequently bring an action under the Civil Rights Act of 1866 (U.S.C. Sec. 1981). Extending the principle to actions based on Title VII, the court pointed out that the claims and the parties were the same at the state and federal	The decision provides a contract with the Supreme Court's decision in Alexander v. Gardner-Denver Co., involving arbitration under a collective bargaining contract (US SupCt-1974, 7 FEP Cases 81). The Supreme Court held that an employee who had pursued a claim of discrimination through the grievance-arbitration procedure under a collective bargaining contract and had lost was not barred from suing in court under Title VII on the same claim. Rights under Title VII are distinctly separate from rights under a collective bargaining contract, the Court said.

Issue	Holding	Comment
Civil Rights Act, Title VII: Procedures—Contd.	levels. (Sinicropi v. Nassau County, CA 2-1979, 19 FEP Cases 1680)	
Suit Notice	An EEOC notice informing a charging party that conciliation efforts had failed and inviting her to request a second, formal notice of right to sue is not itself a "notice of right to sue" that starts the 90-day period for filing an action under Title VII of the Equal Employment Opportunity Act of 1972. The U.S. Court of Appeals for the Eighth Circuit so held in reversing a district court ruling that the 90-day period began to run upon receipt of the first notice from the EEOC. After examining Section 706(f) of the Act, the appeals court concluded that the notice of right to sue should be issued at the completion of the administrative process, and the administrative process is not completed until the EEOC decides not to sue or dismisses the charge. Otherwise, the court stated, the aggrieved person would be required to sue within 90 days or lose his right to sue without knowing whether the EEOC would file suit on his behalf. (Tuft v. McDonnell Douglas Corp., CA 8-1975, 10 FEP Cases 929)	The original Title VII of the Civil Rights Act of 1964 required that the charging party must file a suit within 30 days after receiving the suit notice from the EEOC. The 1972 amendments lengthened the period to 90 days. There have been numerous rulings on the notice requirement, and they often are conflicting. The two-notice procedure was devised by the EEOC prior to the 1972 amendments to overcome the problems faced by many charging parties in obtaining counsel and filing the action before the 30-day period expired. But the courts of appeals established a strict rule on the notice requirement, although the Tenth Circuit held that receipt of the notice, rather than the mailing, triggered the running of the limitation period. (Plunkett v Roadway Express, Inc., CA 10-1974, 8 FEP 817) This decision was handed down under the 1972 Act, but the same principle was applied under the 1964 Act. (Miller v. International Paper Co., CA 5-1969, 1 FEP Cases 647; see also Franks v. Bowman Transport Co., CA 5-1974, 8 FEP Cases 66) There has been a firm rule that failure to file within the limitation period bars the action. (Goodman v. City Products Corp., CA 6-1970, 2 FEP Cases 608; Genovese v. Shell Oil Co., CA 5-1973, 6 FEP Cases 1139; Wong v. The Bon Marche, CA 9-1975, 9 FEP Cases 103)
Timeliness of Filing of Charge With EEOC After Resort to Grievance Procedure	The date of a black employee's discharge, and not the subsequent date on which contractual grievance procedures were concluded, was the final date of the alleged unlawful employment practice for measuring the time within which the employer was required to file a charge with the EEOC, in view of the parties' assumption during the proceedings in the lower courts that the date of discharge was the "final" date. Moreover, the employee's filing of a grievance under the collective bargaining contract did not toll the running of time within which she was required to file a charge with the EEOC. Equitable tolling principles are inapplicable, since the employee was asserting an independent claim based upon a contract right when she pursued the grievance procedures, and she	There was another issue in the case involving whether the increase in the time limit for filing charges with the EEOC, from 90 to 180 days under the Equal Employment Opportunity Act of 1972, applied to the employee's charge that was pending with the EEOC at the time the 1972 Act was enacted. The court held that Congress had the constitutional power to provide for retroactive application of the extended limitations period, and Justices Brennan, Marshall, Stewart, and Stevens said they would reverse the holding of the appeals court on that ground alone without addressing the other issues involved in the case.

Issue	Holding	Comment
Civil Rights Act, Title VII: Procedures—Contd.	was in no way prevented from filing a timely charge with the EEOC. (Electrical Workers v. Robbins & Myers, Inc., US SupCt-1976, 13 FEP Cases 1813)	
Tolling of Action Under 1866 Act	A state statute of limitations applicable to an action under 42 U.S.C. § 1981 (1866 Act) is not tolled by timely filing of charges under Title VII with EEOC, despite the contention that requiring Section 1981 action to be brought while a charge is pending before EEOC would destroy all chances for administrative conciliation and voluntary compliance. A cause of action under Section 1981 is truly independent of that under Title VII, the U.S. Supreme Court stated. (Johnson v. Railway Express Agency, US SupCt-1975, 10 FEP Cases 817)	In making this ruling, the Supreme Court stressed the following: ● An individual who establishes a cause of action under Section 1981 is entitled to both equitable and legal relief, including compensatory and, under certain circumstances, punitive damages. ● A back-pay award under Section 1981 is not restricted to the two-year period specified under Title VII. ● Remedies available under Section 1981 and those available under Title VII, although related and directed to the same ends, are separate, distinct, and independent. Prior to the Supreme Court's ruling in the Johnson case, the U.S. Court of Appeals for the Sixth Circuit had ruled that punitive damages erroneously were awarded to individuals who successfully sued an employer and two unions under both Title VII and 42 U.S.C. § 1981 (1866 Act). The appeals court said that an individual who sues under both the 1866 Act and Title VII does not enlarge his right to relief beyond that authorized by Title VII. A district court had awarded the plaintiffs $4,000,000 in punitive damages against Detroit Edison Co., and $250,000 in punitive damages against Local 223 of the Utility Workers. It denied any damages against Local 17 of the IBEW. The circuit court reversed the punitive-damage awards. (EEOC v. Detroit Edison Co. and Local 223 of the Utility Workers, CA 6-1975, 10 FEP Cases 239) The Supreme Court's decision in the Johnson case appears to cast doubt on the decision of the circuit court in the Detroit Edison case under Section 1981 as well as Title VII.
Trial de Novo: Federal Employees	Employees of the Federal Government who are bringing an action under Title VII have the same right to a trial de novo as is enjoyed by private sector employees and employees of state governments and their political subdivisions, in view of the plain language of Section 717 that	In another case decided the same day, the Supreme Court held that Section 717 is the exclusive individual remedy available to a U.S. Government employee who charges job-related discrimination in violation of Title VII. Congress intended in 1972, the Court said, to

Issue	Holding	Comment
Civil Rights Act, Title VII: Procedures—Contd. Trial de Novo: Federal Employees—Contd.	extended coverage to U.S. Government employees and legislative history of the 1972 amendments to Title VII. However, prior administrative findings may be admitted as evidence in a trial de novo in a court. The decision was unanimous. (Chandler v. Roudebush, US SupCt-1976, 12 FEP Cases 1368)	create exclusive preemptive, administrative, and judicial schemes for redress of discrimination in federal employment. A precisely drawn, detailed statute preempts more general remedies. (Brown v. GSA, US SupCt-1976, 12 FEP Cases 1361)
Civil Rights Act, Title VII: Substantive Rulings Ability Tests: Job Relatedness	The guidelines issued by the EEOC for determining the job-relatedness of employment tests are entitled to "great deference," according to the U.S. Supreme Court. Applying the guidelines, the Court found defects in a company's validation study of tests having a racially disproportionate impact. The validation study, the Court pointed out, compared test scores with subsequent supervisorial rankings of employees that were based on an extremely vague "standard" open to divergent interpretations. So there is no way to determine whether the criteria actually considered were sufficiently related to the employer's legitimate interest in "job-specific ability" to justify the use of the tests. The Court also noted that the validation study dealt only with job-experienced white workers, while the tests themselves are given to new job applicants who are younger, largely inexperienced, and in many instances nonwhite. The EEOC guidelines provide for the generation of separate data for black and white workers, the Court said—for example, a "differential validation" where feasible—and there was no clear showing that differential validation was not feasible for lower level jobs. In any event, the Court concluded, the study would not have validated the employer's tests even if it had been otherwise adequate. There were four concurring opinions on the testing issue and a back-pay issue. Chief Justice Burger both concurred and dissented. He objected to the application of the back-pay principle by the Court, and he also disagreed with the "slavish adherence" to the EEOC guidelines that he contended is required by the Court. Justices Marshall and Rehnquist agreed with the majority opinion by Justice Stewart, but not with some of the things said in the opinion. Justice Blackmun concurred only in the judgment. (Albemarle Paper Co. v. Moody, US SupCt-1975, 10 FEP Cases 1181)	Section 703(h) of the Act allows an employer to act upon the results of "any professionally developed ability test," so long as the test, its administration, or action upon it are not designed, intended, or used to discriminate. The EEOC guidelines take the position that Section 703(h) permits the use only of job-related tests. They hold unlawful an employer's use of educational and testing requirements that are not shown to be job-related and that have a disproportionately adverse effect on blacks. (See below, Griggs v. Duke Power Co.)

Issue	Holding	Comment
Civil Rights Act, Title VII: Substantive Rulings—Contd.	See below under "Back Pay" for another aspect of this case.	
Ability Tests: Job Relatedness—Contd.	An employer's use of ability tests and education standards that are not related to job performance and operate to screen out members of minority groups in hiring and promotion is unlawful under Title VII of the Civil Rights Act of 1964, according to a holding by the U.S. Supreme Court. In a unanimous opinion, the Court upheld the position of the EEOC that tests or standards used in hiring or promoting employees "must measure the person for the job and not the person in the abstract." (Griggs v. Duke Power Co., US SupCt-1971, 3 FEP Cases 175) See below under "Back Pay" for another aspect of this case.	In 1955, nine years before adoption of the Act, the company established a requirement of a high-school education or its equivalent for all employees except those in its labor department. It later amended the promotion and transfer requirements by providing that an employee who was on the payroll prior to September 1, 1965, and who did not have a high-school education or its equivalent could become eligible for transfer or promotion by passing the Wonderlich general intelligence test and the Bennett Mechanical AA general mechanical test with scores equivalent to those achieved by the average high-school graduate. The blacks who filed the suit admitted that the company had abandoned its policy of restricting blacks to the labor department. But they contended that the education and testing requirements preserved and continued the effects of past discrimination, thus violating Title VII.
Ability Tests: Education Standard	An employer did not violate Title VII by using a high school education requirement and aptitude tests for hiring that had a disparate impact on Spanish-surnamed job applicants, since the employer had hired a higher percentage of Spanish-surnamed employees than that found in the labor market. The Tenth Circuit noted also that the employer made statistical adjustments to equalize the raw scores of Spanish-surnamed applicants and Anglo applicants. (EEOC v. Navajo Refining Co., CA 10-1979, 19 FEP Cases 184)	The Tenth Circuit cited Griggs v. Duke Power Co., supra, and Albemarle Paper Co., supra, as requiring the employer to justify the tests as not only job-related but also racially neutral.
Ability Tests: Police Officers—Constitutionality	A personnel test that excludes a disproportionately large number of black applicants for police officer positions does not violate the Fifth Amendment to the Constitution by reason solely of its racially disproportionate impact, since proof of racially discriminatory purpose is necessary for establishing a violation of the equal protection component of the Due Process Clause. The positive relationship found by the district court between the test and performance in the training program was sufficient to validate the test. This conclusion is supported by	The Court also said that black applicants who failed the test, which is neutral on its face and seeks to ascertain whether those who take it have acquired particular levels of verbal skills, can no more successfully claim that the test denied them equal protection than could white applicants who also failed, even with proof that more blacks than whites have been disqualified by the test. The Court added that the conclusion reached was not foreclosed by Griggs v. Duke Power Co., or Albemarle Paper Co. v. Moody, supra.

Issue	Holding	Comment
Civil Rights Act, Title VII: Substantive Rulings—Contd. Ability Tests: Police Officers—Constitutionality—Contd.	regulations of the U.S. Civil Service Commission, by evidence placed before the court, and by the current views of Civil Service Commissioners. The legal standards applicable to actions under Title VII are not applicable to actions under the Fifth or Fourteenth Amendments to the Constitution. Justice Stevens concurred in part, while Justice Stewart joined in Parts I and II of the Court's opinion written by Justice White. (Washington v. Davis, US SupCt-1976, 12 FEP Cases 1415)	
Ability Tests: Teachers' Examinations	In 1978, the Supreme Court, without issuing an opinion, upheld South Carolina's use of the National Teachers Examination in hiring and classifying teachers. The court accepted the standards as professional standards, even though they were in conflict with the EEOC guidelines. Justice White, however, wrote a dissenting opinion in which Justice Brennan joined. The dissent observed that the state used the test, despite the advice of its authors that the test should not be used as the state was using it, and despite the fact that it served to disqualify a greater proportion of black applicants than white applicants and to place a greater percentage of black teachers in lower paying classifications. (National Education Association v. State of South Carolina, U.S. v. Same, US SupCt-1978, 16 FEP Cases 501)	
Arrest and Conviction Record: Use in Hiring	An employer violated Title VII by refusing to hire a black job applicant because he had been arrested "on a number of occasions" for offenses other than minor traffic violations. Blacks, the court stated, are arrested substantially more frequently than whites. So any policy that disqualifies prospective employees because they have been arrested once, or more than once, discriminates against black applicants in violation of Title VII. The discrimination exists even though the policy is applied objectively and fairly as between applicants of various races. (Gregory v. Litton Systems, Inc., CA 9-1972, 5 FEP Cases 267)	The district court had awarded the black applicant both damages and injunctive relief. (Gregory v. Litton Systems, USDC CCalif-1970, 2 FEP Cases 821) The appeals court, however, struck the injunctive relief, pointing out that the plaintiff was not seeking prospective relief and that the employer had not been shown to have a history of discrimination.
	Refusal by a railroad to consider applicants for employment who had been convicted of a crime more serious than a minor traffic offense violated Title VII of the Civil Rights Act of 1964.	The line of decisions dealing with arrest records and convictions as the basis for refusal to hire began in Gregory v. Litton Systems, supra. The same reasoning was applied to

Issue	Holding	Comment
Civil Rights Act, Title VII: Substantive Rulings—Contd. Arrest and Conviction Record: Use in Hiring—Contd.	Such a policy, the U.S. Court of Appeals for the Eighth Circuit ruled, disqualifies disproportionately more black applicants than white applicants. The applicant, who was seeking a clerk's job, had been convicted of refusing military induction. The court below had found no violation by comparing the number of blacks rejected in a 26-month period with the total pool of applicants. It considered the resulting figure of 2.05 percent as showing a de minimis discriminatory effect when compared with the percentage of blacks in the metropolitan area (16 percent). (Green v. Missouri Pacific R.R. Co., USDC EMo-1974, 8 FEP Cases 1029) The appeals court stated that the district court's analysis suffered from two defects: (1) comparison of the number of black applicants rejected because of a conviction record with the total number of black applicants dilutes the discriminatory impact of the policy against blacks; and (2) the issue is whether the policy operates in a disparate manner against blacks, not whether the blacks suffering from the policy are statistically many in number. Since the statistics show that the policy disqualifies black applicants at a substantially higher rate than white applicants, a prima facie case of discrimination has been established. This requires the employer to show that the practice is required by business necessity. Under the business-necessity test, the appeals court said, the challenged practice must have no acceptable alternative that will accomplish the goal of fostering safety and efficiency with a lesser differential racial impact. This the company did not show. (Green v. Missouri Pacific R.R. Co., CA 8-1975, 10 FEP Cases 1409)	discharge for garnishment, the reasoning being that blacks were subject to more garnishment than whites. (Johnson v. Pike Corp., supra) In the public sector, where there are some constitutional obligations, public employers have been ordered by some federal courts not to apply a flat rule forbidding the employment of convicted felons. Modifying a lower court decision, the Eighth Circuit Court of Appeals said that it was persuaded by the arguments of the Minnesota Civil Service Commission that applicants' conviction records, at least in cases of aggravated offenses and multiple offenses and multiple convictions, may have a bearing on the suitability of an applicant from the standpoint of protecting the public and fellow firefighters. But the court added that the Commission could be required to submit for approval a rule providing that, at a minimum, an applicant's conviction record should not be an absolute bar to employment. (Carter v. Gallagher, CA 8-1971, 3 FEP Cases 900) A three-judge federal court in Iowa found that an Iowa statute prohibiting the employment of any convicted felons in any civil service jobs violated the Equal Protection Clause of the U.S. Constitution. The court criticized the lack of consideration given to the nature and seriousness of the crime in relation to the job sought and the degree of rehabilitation. It also objected to the irrebuttable presumption in the statute that conviction of a felony establishes a person's unfitness for civil service employment. (Butts v. Nichols, USDC SIowa-1974, 8 FEP Cases 676) See below under "Reverse Discrimination" for discussion of another aspect of Carter v. Gallagher, supra.
Constitutionality: Title VII Public Sector	The 1972 amendments extending the coverage of Title VII to state and local governments are constitutional. The Eleventh Amendment to the Constitution does not bar the award under Title VII of retroactive retirement benefits and attorneys' fees to individuals who proved that a state retirement system had discriminated against them because of their sex. (1) The Eleventh Amendment is limited by Section 5 of the Fourteenth Amendment, which gives Congress power to enforce the substantive provisions of the Fourteenth Amendment "by appropriate legislation;" and (2) Congress may provide, in	This case took on added significance because of a decision handed down four days earlier holding constitutional the 1974 amendments to the Fair Labor Standards Act that extended minimum-wage and overtime-pay protection to almost all nonsupervisory employees of state and local governments. (National League of Cities v. Usery, US SupCt-1976, 22 WH Cases 1064) For a discussion of the Equal Pay Act, see below under "Equal Pay Act; Constitutionality: Public Sector."

Issue	Holding	Comment
Civil Rights Act, Title VII: Substantive Rulings—Contd. Constitutionality: Title VII Public Sector—Contd.	determining what is "appropriate legislation," for private actions against states or state officials that are constitutionally impermissible in other contexts; and (3) Congress' enactment of Title VII was an exercise of its powers under Section 5. The decision was unanimous. Justice Rehnquist wrote the majority opinion; Justices Brennan and Stevens wrote concurring opinions. (Fitzpatrick v. Bitzer, US SupCt-1976, 12 FEP Cases 1586)	
Garnishment Record: Use in Discharge	The same district court as the one above later held that an employer violated Title VII by discharging a member of a minority group whose wages had been subject to garnishment on several occasions. (Johnson v. Pike Corp. of America, USDC CCalif-1971, 3 FEP Cases 1025)	The employer had a rule authorizing discharge for garnishment of wages, but the court observed that it discriminated against members of minority groups, since they were subject to garnishment more often than whites. In reversing a summary judgement entered by a district court for an employer in a garnishment case, the Eighth Circuit adopted the reasoning of Johnson v. Pike Corp., supra, with respect to the necessity of an employer's establishing business justification for the policy. (Wallace v. Debron Corp., CA 8-1974, 7 FEP Cases 595)
Homosexuals: Discrimination—FBI Employee, Due process	Rules and understandings of the Federal Bureau of Investigation (FBI), expressed primarily in its employee handbook, gave an FBI mailroom employee who was discharged for homosexuality legitimate expectation that his employment would not be terminated for reasons unrelated to his job performance and entitled him to procedural protections of the Due Process Clause of the Fifth Amendment to the Constitution before he could be discharged for reasons purporting to rest upon such a relationship. (Ashton v. Civiletti, CA DC-1979, 20 FEP Cases 1601)	The court found that the FBI had made an implied promise of continued employment based on statements made in the letter of employment and the employee handbook. The FBI claimed the employee had resigned, but he asserted the resignation was coerced by a threat not to provide him with a reference if he did not resign.
Homosexuals: Discrimination—Government Agency	The U.S. Civil Service Commission was warranted in terminating employment of a homosexual employee of the EEOC, since (1) the employee was terminated not because of his status as a homosexual or because of any private acts of sexual preference, but because of his "openly and publicly flaunting of his homosexual way of life and indicating further contin-	Title VII of the Civil Rights Act of 1964 does not specifically mention sexual preference as an unlawful basis of discrimination in employment. Neither the Federal Government nor any state government has adopted a law specifically protecting employees against discrimination because of homosexuality. But several local governments have laws or ordi-

Issue	Holding	Comment
Civil Rights Act, Title VII: Substantive Rulings—Contd. Homosexuals: Discrimination—Government Agency—Contd.	uance of such activities" while identifying himself as an employee of a government agency; (2) CSC found that these activities were such that the general public knowledge of them reflected discredit upon the government and impeded the efficiency of the service by lessening public confidence in the fitness of the government to conduct the public business with which it was entrusted; and (3) there was a rational connection between the facts that the CSC relied upon and the conclusions that it reached. (Singer v. Civil Service Comm., CA 9-1976, 12 FEP Cases 208)	nances protecting individuals against employment discrimination based on sexual "preference," "orientation," or "deviation." The most comprehensive local law is that adopted by the District of Columbia in 1973. This law forbids employment discrimination "for any reason other than that of individual merit." The forbidden bases of discrimination include, but are not limited to, the following: "race, color, religion, national origin, sex, age, marital status, personal appearance, sexual orientation, family responsibilities, matriculation, political affiliation, physical handicap, source of income, and place of residence or business."
Homosexuals: Discrimination—Off Duty Conduct	The U.S. Civil Service Commission improperly upheld the discharge of an employee of the National Aeronautics and Space Administration (NASA) who, while off duty, made a homosexual advance to another person, since the record did not suggest any reasonable connection between the evidence against the employee and the "efficiency of the service." CSC found that the employee engaged in immoral conduct and possessed personality traits that rendered him unsuitable for further government employment, but NASA failed to show that the employee's embarrassing conduct threatened the quality of its performance. (Norton v. Macy, CA DC-1969, 9 FEP Cases 1382)	A similar ruling in a later case brought as a class action on behalf of persons whom the U.S. Civil Service Commission would deem unfit for government for the sole reason that employment of a homosexual person might bring the government into "public contempt" led the CSC to abandon its policy of automatic disqualification of known homosexuals. (Society for Individual Rights v. Hampton, USDC NCalif-1973, 11 FEP Cases 1243)
Homosexuals: Discrimination—Sexual Preference	Title VII's ban on sex discrimination applies only to discrimination on the basis of gender, and it should not be judicially extended to include sexual preference such as homosexuality. The court rejected the agrument that discrimination against homosexuals disproportionately affects men because of the highter incidence of homosexuality among men than among women and because of the greater visibility of male homosexuals. One of the three judges dissented. (DeSantis v. Pacific T & T Co., CA 9-1979, 19 FEP Cases 1493)	The court also rejected a contention that the employer, a nursery school, violated Title VII when it terminated a male employee for wearing an earring to school, notwithstanding a contention that the school relied on a stereotype that a man should have a virile, rather than an effeminate appearance. Discrimination because of effeminacy does not fall within the purview of Title VII.
Homosexuals: Discrimination—State Laws	In a case involving California's Constitution, Public Utilities Code, labor Code, and Fair Employment Practice Act, the California Supreme Court handed down the following rulings relating to homosexuals:	The case was a class action filed by four individuals and two associations against the Pacific Telegraph and Telephone Co. and the California Fair Employment Practice Commission. The class consisted of homosexuals

Issue	Holding	Comment
Civil Rights Act, Title VII: Substantive Rulings—Contd. Homosexuals: Discrimination—State Laws—Contd.	• An allegation that a telephone company arbtrarily discriminated against homosexuals seeking employment stated a claim under the equal protection guarantee of the California Constitution, since this provision bars a public utility, which enjoys a state protected monopoly or quasimonopoly, from engaging in arbitrary employment discrimination on grounds unrelated to a person's qualifications. • The Section of the Public Utilities code that forbids a utility to subject any corporation or person "to any prejudice or disadvantage" prohibits a telephone company from engaging in arbitrary employment discrimination against homosexuals. There is no merit in the contention that this provision should be limited to rate or service-oriented discrimination. • Individuals and organizations claiming that an employer discriminates in employment against persons who identify themselves as homosexuals or who are identified with activist homosexual organizations stated a cause of action against the employer for interfering with their political freedom in violation of the Labor Code provisions forbidding an employer to (1) adopt a policy tending to control or direct political activities or affiliations of employees, and (2) attempt to coerce or influence employees to refrain from adopting a particular line or course of political activity. These provisions are not confined to partisan political activity, and the struggle of the homosexual community for equal rights, particularly in the field of employment, must be recognized as political activity. • The ban on sex discrimination in the Fair Employment Practice Act does not encompass homosexuals, notwithstanding a contention that the Act should be construed to bar all forms of arbitrary discrimination. • The ban on sex discrimination in the Fair Employment Practice Act does not encompass homosexuals, notwithstanding the contention that discrimination against homosexuals is in effect discrimination based on the gender of the homosexual's partner. The legislature did not contemplate discrimination against homosexuals when it proscribed discrimination on the basis of sex, and the Fair Employment Practice Commission consistently has refused to accept	who are past, present, or future applicants for employment by the company. The decision was by a two-to-one margin. The dissenting Justice pointed out that the majority conceded that the Fair Employment Practice Act did not apply to homosexuals, but nonetheless, relying on constitutional and statutory provisions "having no bearing whatever on the subject of the employment of homosexuals," concluded that the complaint stated a cause of action against the company. A related case decided by the Ninth Circuit, Desantis v. Pacific T&T Co., supra, is discussed above under "Homosexuals: Discrimination—Sex."

Issue	Holding	Comment
Civil Rights Act, Title VII: Substantive Rulings—Contd. Homosexuals: Discrimination—State Laws—Contd.	jurisdiction over complaints charging discrimination based on sexual orientation. ● The Fair Employment Practice Act does not unconstitutionally deny homosexuals equal protection of the law, even though it forbids discrimination on the basis of such factors as race, religion, and sex, but not on the basis of homosexuality. The Act is not unconstitutional simply because the legislature declined to extend its remedies to all potentially aggrieved groups. (Gay Law Students Ass'n v. Pacific T&T Co., Calif. SupCt-1979, 19 FEP Cases 1419)	
Homosexuals: Discrimination—Teacher	A school teacher who was transferred from teaching to an administrative position after school officials learned that he was a homosexual may not challenge his transfer as unconstitutional in view of his intentional omission on his employment application of information concerning his membership in a college organization of homosexuals, even though the school officials would not have employed him if they had known of his membership in the organization. (Acafora v. Board of Education of Montgomery County, CA 4-1974, 9 FEP Cases 1287)	The employee not only attended meetings of the homosexual oranization, but he also served as its treasurer and joined other members in a lawsuit that established it as an official university organization.
Management Positions	The significant underrepresentation of blacks in supervisory-level management positions at a company's plant was an adequate basis for invalidating the company's "total assessment" program governing employees who bid for promotion to "critical" nonmanagement jobs and management jobs. The Fifth Circuit so decided in affirming a federal district court's holding. The program required the use of criteria that involved substantial subjectivity and provided management personnel the opportunity to choose which events to emphasize or omit, the court explained. (Fisher v. Procter & Gamble Mfg. Co., CA 5-1980, 22 FEP Cases 356)	The court noted that at the time the action was filed, one of 63 management positions at the plant was held by a black employee, while blacks comprised 11.8 percent of the total work force.
Methadone Addiction	A general policy of excluding all methadone users from employment with the New York City Transit Authority was upheld by the Supreme Court. Since the policy rationally serves the objectives of safety and efficiency, the Court	All the dissenting justices took the position that the statistics are sufficient to establish a prima facie case of racial discrimination in violation of Title VII. Justices White and Marshall also take the position that a classifi-

Issue	Holding	Comment
Civil Rights Act, Title VII: Substantive Rulings—Contd. Methadone Addiction—Contd.	said, it violates neither Title VII of the Civil Rights Act of 1964 nor the Equal Protection Clause of the Fourteenth Amendment. The district court which tried the case relied on two statistics in finding that the requirement had a racially discriminatory effect: 81 percent of the employees referred to the TA's medical director for suspected drug violations were either black or Hispanic, and 63 percent of those receiving methadone maintenance in public programs were black or Hispanic. In an opinion by Justice Stevens, the court found the statistics "weak," and, even if they were capable of establishing a prima facie case of discrimination, they were sufficiently rebutted by the TA's demonstration that the methadone policy is job-related. The Federal district court's express finding that the policy was not motivated by racial reasons forecloses any claim in rebuttal that it was mere pretext for intentional discrimination. Justices Brennan, White, and Marshall dissented. Justice Powell concurred in part and dissented in part. (NYC Transit Authority v. Beazer, US SupCt-1979, 19 FEP Cases 149)	cation that treats all persons who successfully are on methadone maintenance different from the general population is unjustified, irrational, and insidious and violates the Equal Protection Clause.
National Origin Discrimination	A Mexican-American planning analyst made out a prima facie case of national origin discrimination, the U.S. Court of Appeals for the Eight Circuit decided, reversing a lower court decision. The court observed that the employee had not been promoted for 15 years, although his work often was praised by supervisory personnel. On three occasions, he was the only eligible employee denied the opportunity to attend company training programs. (Marquez v. Omaha District Sales Office, CA 8-1971, 3 FEP Cases 275)	The holding reversed one by a federal district court that found that the employer had not been guilty of any past or present discrimination. (Marquez v. Omaha District Sales Office, USDC Neb-1970, 2 FEP Cases 983)
National Origin Discrimination: Citizenship	An employer's long-standing practice of not hiring aliens was held by the Supreme Court not to violate the Title VII prohibition against employment discrimination based on national origin. (Espinoza v. Farah Manufacturing Co., US SupCt-1973, 6 FEP Cases 933)	In the view of the Court, the term "national origin" was not intended to embrace citizenship requirements. Justice Douglas dissented.
National Origin Discrimination: Citizenship—Act of 1866	After the Espinoza decision, an action was filed by a registered alien against an employer and a union under both Title VII and 42 U.S.C. § 1981 (passed in 1866). Although the court held that the alleged discrimination did not violate	Prior to the Guerra case, the Supreme Court held that the Equal Protection Clause of the U.S. Constitution barred a state from excluding an alien from the state's competitive civil service. (Sugarman v. Dougall, US SupCt-

Issue	Holding	Comment
Civil Rights Act, Title VII: Substantive Rulings—Contd. National Origin Discrimination: Citizenship—Act of 1866—Contd.	Title VII, it violated Section 1981 as discriminating against Spanish-surnamed Americans or persons of Mexican origin. (Guerra v. Manchester Terminal Corp., CA 5-1974, 8 FEP Cases 433)	1973, 5 FEP Cases 1152) This principle later was extended by an appeals court to hold unconstitutional the U.S. Civil Service Commission's regulation forbidding the employment of aliens. (Wong v. Hampton, CA 9-1974, 7 FEP Cases 58) Although the term "national origin" is not defined in Title VII or other federal statutes relating to job description, it has come to mean the country of one's ancestry, rather than race or color. The majority of cases so far have involved Spanish-surnamed Americans—a group including Mexican-Americans, Puerto Ricans, and others of Spanish heritage.
	An employer did not violate Title VII's ban on national origin discrimination when it discharged a bilingual Spanish-surnamed employee for violating a rule requiring employees to speak in English in public areas while on the job, where the rule did not apply to conversations during breaks or other employee free-time. (Garcia v. Gloor, CA 5-1980, 22 FEP Cases 1403)	The court also held that since the discharge did not violate Title VII, the employee could not obtain relief under the Civil Rights Acts of 1866 and 1871 (42 U.S.C. §§ 1981, 1985(c))
	The Civil Rights Act of 1866 (42 U.S.C. §§ 1981), which gives all persons the same rights as are enjoyed by "white citizens," applies to a claim by a former employee that because of his Mexican-American descent, his employer treated him differently from Anglo employees and his union failed to represent him as it had represented its Anglo members. The Act is directed to racial discrimination primarily, the Tenth Circuit stated, but is is not necessarily limited to the technical or restrictive meaning of "race." If "white citizens" means a race, the court added, it would appear that members of a group that are discriminated against because they are somehow different, as compared with "white citizens" is within the scope of the statute. (Manzanares v. Safeway Stores, CA 10-1979, 19 FEP Cases 191)	The prejudice against the former employee, the Tenth Circuit observed, is directed against persons with Spanish surnames. This is a group whose rights can be measured against the standard group or control group.
National Origin Discrimination: Citizenship—Constitutionality (Civil Service)	A U.S. Civil Service Commission regulation that indiscriminately excluded all aliens from all civil service positions is unconstitutional as depriving resident aliens of liberty without due process of law in violation of the Fifth Amendment to the Constitution. Since resident aliens are admitted into the U.S. as a result of	In a later per curiam order, the Supreme Court affirmed a three-judge federal court's holding that the same Civil Service Commission regulation was unconstitutional as violating the Fifth Amendment to the Constitution. (US SupCt-1976, 12 FEP Cases 1446; decision below, Ramos v. Civil Service Commission,

Issue	Holding	Comment
Civil Rights Act, Title VII: Substantive Rulings—Contd. National Origin Discrimination: Citizenship—Constitutionality (Civil Service)—Contd.	decisions made by Congress and the President, implemented by the Immigration Service acting under the U.S. Attorney General, due process requires that deprivation of such an important liberty be made either at a comparable level of government or, if it is permitted to be made by the Civil Service Commission, that it be justified by reasons that are a proper concern of that agency. (Hampton v. Wong, US SupCt-1976, 12 FEP Cases 1377)	USDC PR-1974, 10 FEP Cases 55)
National Origin Discrimination: Citizenship—Constitutionality (State Law)	The New York statute requiring state troopers to be U.S. citizens bears a rational relationship to special demands of the police function, which includes enforcement and execution of governmental policy, and therefore does not violate rights of aliens under the Equal Protection Clause of the Fourteenth Amendment to the U.S. Constitution. Justice Stewart concurred and Justice Blackmun concurred in the result. Justices Marshall, Brennan, and Stevens dissented. (Foley v. Connelie, US SupCt-1978, 17 FEP Cases 1)	The majority took the view that a state that excludes aliens from employment as state troopers need show only some rational relationship between the interest sought to be protected and classification based on alienage.
National Origin Discrimination: Citizenship—Constitutionality, (Teachers)	A New York statute forbidding the permanent certification as public schooi teachers of aliens who have not manifested an intention to apply for U.S. Citizenship does not violate the Equal Protection Clause of the Fourteenth Amendment. A majority of the Supreme Court found that the citizenship requirement rationally serves the state's educational goals. Teachers play a critical part in developing students' attitudes toward government and an understanding of the role of government in society. The decision was by a five-to-four margin, with Justices Blackmun joined by Justices Brennan, Marshall and Stevens dissenting. (Ambach v. Norwick, US SupCt-1979, 19 FEP Cases 467)	The dissenting opinion argued that the statute is overbroad and irrational. Moreover, it asserted that it is "logically impossible" to differentiate between teachers, who, the majority said, can be required to be citizens, and attorneys, who, the Court held several years ago, could not be required to be citizens. (In re Griffiths, US SupCt-1973, 413 U.S. 717) The dissent also distinguished Sugarman v. Dougall, infra, as involving a citizenship requirement only for a narrowly defined class oppositions.
Past Discrimination: Affirmative Relief	Section 703(j) of Title VII, which forbids "preferential treatment" solely because of racial imbalance, must be read in conjunction with the fundamental purposes of the Act and the provision for affirmative relief. So Section 703(j) "cannot be construed as a ban on affirmative relief against continuation of effects of past discrimination resulting from present practices (neutral on their face) which have the practical effect of continuing past injustices. Any other	The appeals court noted that continued discrimination could result from such past practices as a limitation of new apprentices to relatives of the all-white membership of a union or limitation of membership to persons who had previous experience under the union contract, if such experience was racially limited to whites.

Issue	Holding	Comment
Civil Rights Act, Title VII: Substantive Rulings—Contd. Past Discrimination: Affirmative Relief—Contd.	interpretation would allow complete nullification of the stated purposes" of the Act. Following this reasoning, the Sixth Circuit reversed a federal district court's refusal to order affirmative relief in a pattern-or-practice action brought by the U.S. Attorney General against a union. (U.S. v. IBEW, Local 38, CA 6-1970, 2 FEP Cases 716, cert. denied, US SupCt-1970, 2 FEP Cases 1121)	
		The scope of the affirmative relief that may be granted was illustrated by the settlement agreement between the Labor Department and the EEOC, on the one hand, and the AT&T and the Bell system companies, on the other. Among other things, the agreement required the companies to do the following: ● Make payments of about $15 million to 13,000 women and 2,000 minority men denied pay and promotion opportunities. ● Establish a new promotion and wage adjustment policy that will increase wages for many employees by about $23 million a year. ● Develop goals for increasing the utilization of women and minorities in each job classification within the system. ● Establish goals for the employment of males in previously all female jobs. (For the text of the consent order in the AT&T case, see FEP Manual 431:73.)
	In determining whether racial discrimination that occurred prior to the effective date of Title VII is perpetuated in current employment practices, it may be necessary to go back as many as five decades, according to the Fifth Circuit. The court issued detailed guidelines for an order to remedy racial discrimination in a railroad terminal. In remanding the case, the appeals court told the lower court to consider, among other things, the toal employment picture at the terminal. (U.S. v. Jacksonville Terminal Co., CA 5-1971, 3 FEP Cases 862, petition for rehear'g denied. CA 5-1971, 4 FEP Cases 2, cert. denied, US SupCt-1972, 4 FEP Cases 661)	The case was a "pattern or practice" action filed by the Justice Department against the company. The lower court ruled aganst the government on all the charges. (U.S. v. Jacksonville Terminal Co., USDC MFLa-1970, 2 FEP Cases 611, aff'd and reman'd in part, CA 5-1971, 3 FEP Cases 862: petition for rehearing denied, CA 5-1971, 4 FEP Cases 2, cert. denied, US SupCt-1972, 4 FEP Cases 661)
Past Discrimination: Seniority Systems—Constructive Seniority	Section 703(k) of Title VII contains an exemption from the discrimination prohibition for "bona fide" seniority systems. This raised the question whether a "bona fide" seniority system	Prior to the Bowman decision, a number of circuit courts had upheld plant-wide or company-wide seniority systems as bona fide under Section 703(h). The systems applied the

Issue	Holding	Comment
Civil Rights Act, Title VII: Substantive Rulings—Contd. Past Discrimination: Seniority Systems—Constructive Seniority—Contd.	insulates an employer and a union against discrimination charges, even though the system may be discriminatory in effect. During its 1976-1977 term, the Supreme Court handed down a landmark decision on the interplay between Title VII and contractual seniority systems. It ruled as follows: Blacks who were hired by a trucking company only for city-driving jobs and who were not permitted to transfer to over-the-road driving jobs were unlawfully discriminated against. The remedy found appropriate was to award them retroactive seniority back to the date of applicaton for over-the-road jobs; this would put the black drivers in their "rightful places." Such relief may be denied, the Court added, only on the basis of "unusual" and adverse impact on other employees. (Franks v. Bowman Transportation Co., US SupCt-1976, 12 FEP Cases 549)	"last-hired, first-fired" principle. The Seventh Circuit did so in Waters v. Wisconsin Steel Works, CA 7-1974, 8 FEP Cases 577; the Third Circuit in Jersey Central Power and Light Co. v. IBEW, CA 3-1975, 9 FEP Cases 117; the Fifth Circuit in Watkins v. Steelworkers, CA 5-1975, 10 FEP Cases 1297; and the Second Circuit in Chance v. Board of Examiners, CA 2-1976, 11 FEP Cases 1450. See below for a discussion of the modification of the Chance decision on rehearing.
	Following the principle of the Franks case, the Second Circuit granted the relief of constructive seniority to persons who had taken and failed discriminatory examinations for supervisory positions and to those who had failed to apply for the examinations or failed to take them because they reasonably believed the examinations to be discriminatory and unrelated to job performance. (Chance v. Board of Examiners, CA 2-1976, 13 FEP Cases 150)	The decision was handed down on a petition for rehearing of an earlier decision in which the court had upheld a facially neutral plan of "excessing" or removing employees pursuant to the concept of "last hired-first fired." (Chance v. Board of Examiners, CA 2-1976, 11 FEP Cases 1451) In addition to the Franks' decision, the Second Circuit cited a decision by another panel of the same court applying the principle of constructive seniority adopted in the Franks' case. (Acha v. Beame, CA 2-1976, 12 FEP Cases 257) Upon reconsideration in the light of the Supreme Court's decisions in Teamsters v. U.S., infra, and Evans v. United Airlines, infra, the district court held that the discriminatees were limited to a revised seniority date no earlier than March 24, 1972—the date of extension of Title VII to municipal employees. (Acha v. Beame, USDC SNY-1977, 15 FEP Cases 413), aff'd CA 2-1978, 16 FEP Cases 526)
Past Discrimination: Seniority Systems—Union Violations	The Eighth Circuit in a case decided prior to Teamsters v. U.S., infra, issued a broad remedial order directing local unions to take a number of steps, including opening hiring halls to qualified blacks, modifying experience requirements for otherwise qualified blacks, modifying the journeyman's examination procedure, and adjusting initiation fees. (U.S. v. Sheet Metal	Prior to the Teamsters decision, courts also had issued broad remedial orders against employers to eliminate present effects of past discrimination. (See, for example, Local 189 Papermakers and Paperworkers, CA 5-1969, 1 FEP Cases 875, cert. denied by US SupCt-1970, 2 FEP Cases 426; U.S. v. Continental Can Co., USDC EVa-1970, 2 FEP Cases 1044)

Issue	Holding	Comment
Civil Rights Act, Title VII: Substantive Rulings—Contd. Past Discrimination: Seniority Systems-Union Violations—Contd.	Workers, CA 8-1969, 2 FEP Cases 127) The Fifth Circuit also approved a broad remedial order against a union that restricted membership to sons or close relatives of present members and refused to refer blacks or Mexican-Americans for employment. The order required the union to admit four persons to membership, to refer nine others for employment, and to alternate white and black referrals until objective membership criteria are developed. (Local 53, International Association of Heat and Frost Insulators and Asbestos Workers v. Vogler, CA 5-1969, 1 FEP Cases 577)	
Past Discrimination: Seniority Systems—Upheld as Bona Fide	In 1977, the Supreme Court significantly qualified the doctrine. Again, members of minority groups were hired only for city-driving jobs, and separate seniority rosters were maintained. A city-driver hired for an over-the-road job forfeited his accumulated seniority and started at the bottom of the list for over-the-road seniority. The discriminatory hiring practices were reinforced by a discriminatory transfer policy. Only white city-drivers were permitted to transfer to over-the-road jobs. In upholding the system, the Supreme Court relied on the Section 703(h) exemption for bona fide seniority systems. A seniority system that is adopted without a discriminatory motive, the court said, is insulated from attack by Section 703(h). The fact that the system perpetuates pre-Act discrimination, even post-Act discrimination, does not affect its bona fide status. Section 703(h) immunizes all bona fide seniority systems. It does not distinguish between the perpetuation of pre-Act discrimination and post-Act discrimination. (Teamsters v. U.S. (T.I.M.E.-D.C., Inc.) 14 FEP Cases 1514)	The Teamsters' decision made some far-reaching changes in the interpretation of Title VII as applied by the courts below. Here are the principal changes: ● What had been treated as departmental seniority must be treated as hiring and transfer determination. A number of lower court decisions had required employers and unions to replace a departmental or craft seniority with plant-wide seniority. ● To obtain financial or seniority relief, the plaintiffs must establish that they were subject to post-Act hiring or transfer discrimination. Prior to the Supreme Court's decision, lower courts had awarded plaintiffs back pay, preferential transfer, and adjustment of seniority where it was found that an employer and a union had maintained a seniority policy that perpetuated any prior discrimination unless compelled by business necessity.
	In a case decided the same day as the Teamsters' case, the court added a new point to the doctrine. An airline discharged a stewardess in 1968 pursuant to its policy of not employing married stewardesses. The policy was abandoned in 1972 and the stewardess was rehired. In 1973, more than one year later, she filed a charge with the EEOC, alleging that the company's policy of refusing to credit prior service for seniority was unlawful as perpetuating prior discrimination. The court rejected the claim on two grounds.	Later, in a case brought under both Title VII and the 1866 Act, the Fourth Circuit Court of Appeals held that a holding that a seniority system that is lawful under Title VII precludes a holding that the same seniority system is unlawful under the 1866 Act. (Johnson v. Ryder Truck Lines, CA 4-1978, 17 FEP Cases 571) The decision was denied review by the Supreme Court. (19 FEP Cases 467)

Issue	Holding	Comment
Civil Rights Act, Title VII: Substantive Rulings—Contd. Past Discrimination: Seniority Systems—Upheld as Bona Fide—Contd.	● First, it said the seniority system, which based seniority solely on current employment, was bona fide and so was protected by Section 703(h). ● Second, the court pointed out that the charge was not filed within 90 days of the alleged violation (the time limit was raised to 180 days in 1972, but the Court said the 90-day limit was applicable). So it decided the case should be dismissed. (United Airlines v. Evans, US SupCt-1977, 14 FEP Cases 1510)	
	A provision of a multi-employer contract that temporary employees must work 45 weeks in one calendar year to attain permanent status and greater benefits is a component of a "seniority system" within the meaning of Section 703(h) of the Civil Rights Act of 1964; the provision does not directly accord benefits based on length of service, but it does establish a threshhold requirement for entering the permanent employee seniority track. (Calif. Brewers Assn. v. Bryant, US SupCt, 1980, 22 FEP Cases 1)	The Fourth Circuit has found that Section 703(h), which permits employers to make employment decisions on the basis of a bona fide seniority system, is inapplicable to seniority systems that did not exist when Title VII became effective in 1965. (Patterson v. American Tobacco Co., CA 4, 1980, 24 FEP Cases 531)
Pensioners: Right to Sue Under Act	A discharged employee's successful application for a pension under an industry-wide agreement does not deprive him of standing to bring an action against his former employer and his union under Title VII, according to the U.S. Court of Appeals for the Third Circuit. A lower court had dismissed the action on the ground that the pensioner was not an "employee" under Title VII. But the Appeals Court states that a person dos not have to be an "employee" to sue under Title VII. It is sufficient if he is a person "claiming to be aggrieved." (Hackett v. McGuire Bros., Inc., CA 3-1971, 3 FEP Cases 648)	In opposing the action, the employer and the union cited the Pittsburgh Plate Glass decision in which retirees were held not be "employees" under the Taft-Hartley Act. (NLRB v. Pittsburgh Plate Glass Co., US SupCt-1971, 78 LRRM 2974)
Preemption: Contract Remedies	Contractual grievance procedures need not be exhausted before a charge is filed with the Equal Employment Opportunity Commission under Title VII of the Act. Nor need contract procedures be exhausted before an employee files an action in court for injunctive relief and damages under Title VII. (King v. Georgia Power Co., USDC NGa-1968, 69 LRRM 2094, 1 FEP Cases 357; Culpepper v. Reynolds Metals Co., USDC NGa-1968, 70 LRRM 2360, 1 FEP Cases 590)	In a non-Title VII case, the Supreme Court previously had held that black and white employees could maintain an action for an injunction and damages against a railroad and a union for their refusal to promote them because of alleged racial discrimination, even though the employees had failed to exhaust their remedies under the contract, the union constitution, and the Railway Labor Act. The employees alleged that the refusal to promote violated the contract and the union's duty of

Issue	Holding	Comment
Civil Rights Act, Title VII: Substantive Rulings—Contd.		fair representation. The court found that it would have been futile for employees to proceed with the contract and statutory remedies. (Glover v. St. Louis-San Francisco Ry., US SupCt-1969, 70 LRRM 2097)
Preemption: Contract Procedures—Prior Arbitration	The doctrine of election of remedies, the doctrine of waiver, and the federal labor policy favoring arbitration do not act as a bar to a suit under Title VII of the Civil Rights Act of 1964 by a discharged employee whose claim of racial discrimination was rejected by an arbitrator. This unanimous decision of the Supreme Court reversed the U.S. Court of Appeals for the Tenth Circuit. The Court also ruled that a federal court is not required to honor the arbitrator's award, but instead should consider the employee's claim de novo. (Alexander v. Gardner-Denver Co., US SupCt-1974, 7 FEP Cases 81) In reaching its conclusion, the Court reasoned that Title VII was designed to supplement, rather than supplant, existing laws and institutions relating to employment discriminaton. Rejecting the election-of-remedies doctrine, the Court pointed out that an employee submitting a grievance to arbitration seeks to vindicate his contractual rights, whereas his Title VII action concerns independent statutory rights accorded by Congress. The distinctly separate nature of these rights is not vitiated merely because both were violated as a result of the same factual occurrence, and no inconsistency results from permitting both rights to be enforced in their respectively appropriate forums. The Court also ruled that there can be no prospective waiver of an employee's rights under Title VII, and the submission of the grievance to arbitration does not alter the situation. Upon remand of the Alexander case, the plaintiff's claim of racial discrimination was denied and the Supreme Court denied review. (Alexander v. Gardner-Denver Co., CA 10-1975, 11 FEP Cases 149, cert. denied by US SupCt-1976, 11 FEP Cases 1450)	During the argument, the employer proposed that the Court adopt a rule setting forth standards for district courts to defer to arbitration awards, as had been done by the Fifth Circuit in the Rios case. (Rios v. Reynolds Metals Co., CA 5-1972, 5 FEP Cases 1) The Supreme Court refused, stating that arbitration procedures are inappropriate for the resolution of rights created by Title VII. But it did add that an award can be admitted into evidence and given such weight as would seem appropriate. Moreover, in footnote 21 it noted that, although it is adopting no standards for determining the weight to be given an arbitration award, it does list a number of relevant factors that might be considered by courts in giving weight to arbitrators' awards. The Court's holding resolved a conflict among a number of appeals court decisions. In the Dewey case, the Sixth Circuit held that a grievant waived his right to a remedy in the federal courts under Title VII by seeking to obtain redress for the alleged racial discrimination under the grievance-arbitraton provisions of the collective bargaining contract. (Dewey v. Reynolds Metals Co., CA 6-1970, 2 FEP Cases 687) But the Fifth Circuit held there was no waiver in the Hutchings case. (Hutchings v. U.S. Industries, Inc., CA 5-1970, 2 FEP Cases 725) The Seventh Circuit followed the Hutchings reasoning in the Rose case. (Rose v. Bridgeport Brass Co., CA 7-1973, 6 FEP Cases 837) In the Bowe case, the Seventh Circuit earlier had held that a party may pursue both contractual and statutory remedies, but must elect which remedy to take after adjudication to preclude duplicate relief. (Bowe v. Colgate Palmolive Co., CA 7-1969, 2 FEP Cases 121) The decision in the Dewey case was affirmed by the Supreme Court by an equally divided vote (Justice Harlan not participating). This convinced the Sixth Circuit that the employee could pursue both contractual and statutory remedies in the Avco case. (Newman v. Avco Corp., CA 6-1971, 3 FEP Cases 1137) The same court expressed a

Issue	Holding	Comment
Civil Rights Act, Title VII: Substantive Rulings—Contd. Preemption: Contract Procedures—Prior Arbitration—Contd.		conflicting view in the later Spann case. (Spann v. Joanna Mills Co., CA 6-1971, 3 FEP Cases 831) The confusion stemmed from the fact that Dewey included a religious issue as well as the arbitration issue, and the four-to-four split in the Supreme Court may have been on the religious issue, as demonstrated by the Alexander decision.
	In a case decided while Gardner-Denver was pending before the Supreme Court, the U.S. Court of Appeals at Chicago ruled that an employee who unsuccessfully claimed in an arbitration proceeding that there termination violated a collective bargaining contract could not litigate the matter again in an action under Title VII. (Rose v. Bridgeport Brass Co., CA 7-1973, 6 FEP Cases 837)	The case involved a female employee on sick leave who asserted that the employer's failure to reinstate her constituted sex discrimination.
	Late in 1972, the U.S. Court of Appeals for the Fifth Circuit set forth the conditions under which a court may defer to an arbitration award in a Title VII action. They are: (1) the contractual right coincides with rights under Title VII, (2) the arbitrator's decision is in no way violative of private rights guaranteed by Title VII or of public policy that inheres in Title VII, (3) the factual issues before the court are identical to those decided by the arbitrator, (4) the arbitrator had the power under the contract to decide the ultimate issue of discrimination, (5) the evidence presented at the arbitration hearing dealt adequately with all factual issues, (6) the arbitrator actually decided the factual issues presented to the court, and (7) the arbitration proceeding was fair, regular, and free of procedural irregularities. (Rios v. Reynolds Metals Co., CA 5-1972, 5 FEP Cases 1)	Although this decision was handed down before the Supreme Court's Alexander v. Gardner-Denver holding, supra, it still may have significance in the light of Footnote 21 in Gardner-Denver, which lists a number of relevant factors that might be considered by courts in giving weight to arbitrator's awards.
Preemption: Railway Labor Act	The Railway Labor Act did not preempt the right of black train porters to maintain an action under Title VII of the Civil Rights Act of 1964 against a railroad that allegedly discriminated against them on the basis of race by classifying them only as porters. The porters contended that the railroad was not according them equal employment opportunities, equal opportunites for advancement, or compensation equal to that of substantially all white brakemen, who did almost the same work. (Norman	The decision vacated a district court decision holding that the jurisdiction of the porters to sue under Title VII was preempted by the Railway Labor Act. (Norman v. Missouri Pacific Railroad, USDC EArk-1968, 1 FEP Cases 331)

Issue	Holding	Comment
Civil Rights Act, Title VII: Substantive Rulings—Contd.	v. Missouri Pacific Railroad, CA 8-1969, 1 FEP Cases 863)	
Preemption: State Safety Laws	A state regulation limiting lifting by female employees to 30 pounds was not a defense to an action by a female employee for damages and an injunction because she was denied a job as a switchman because she was a female. The court noted that the EEOC had recognized certain state protective laws as bona fide occupational qualifications, but it agreed with the employee that the 30-pound limit was too inflexible and too low. (Weeks v. Southern Bell Telephone Co., CA 5-1969, 70 LRRM 2843, 1 FEP Cases 656; see above under "Attorneys' Fees" for a further discussion of this case.) In a similar holding, the U.S. Court of Appeals at Chicago held that a limit of 35 pounds on weight to be lifted by female employees amounted to unlawful discrimination based on sex. (Bowe v. Colgate-Palmolive Co., CA 7-1969, 2 FEP Cases 121)	Section 703(e)(1) provides an exception to the prohibitions against discrimination based on religion, sex, or national origin where one of the three is a "bona fide occupational qualification." On this basis, state laws limiting hours and weights to be lifted by women have been asserted as defenses to Title VII discrimination charges. This contention was rejected in a case in which a woman sought a job as a railroad agent-telegrapher. (Rosenfeld v. Southern Pacific Co., CA 9-1971, 3 FEP Cases 604) The court found that the state rules limiting hours and weights for female employees were preempted by Title VII and enjoined the employer from relying upon them to discriminate against female employees. Also see Mengelkoch v. Industrial Welfare Commission, USDC CCalif-1968, 68 LRRM 2277, 1 FEP Cases 314, in which a three-judge federal court first held that such problems of interpretation of state laws should be resolved first by state courts. The Supreme Court later reversed and remanded the decision. (Mengelkoch v. Welfare Commission, US SupCt-1968, 3 FEP Cases 55) The U.S. Court of Appeals for the Ninth Circuit then held that the district court erred in not determining whether Title VII superseded the California Act regulating hours of work for women. (Mengelkoch v. Welfare Commission, CA 9-1971, 3 FEP Cases 471)
Preemption: Taft-Hartley Act	The jurisdiction of federal district courts in actions to enjoin or recover damages for racial discrimination in violation of Title VII is not preempted by the Taft-Hartley Act. (See Local 53, International Association of Heat and Frost Insulators and Asbestos Workers v. Vogler, CA 5-1969, 70 LRRM 2257, 1 FEP Cases 577; King v. Georgia Power Co., USDC NGa-1968, 69 LRRM 2094, 1 FEP Cases 357; Dobbins v. Local 212, IBEW, USDC SOhio-1968, 69 LRRM 2313, 1 FEP Cases 387)	For some time, it appeared as if there would be considerable overlapping of jurisdiction under Title VII and the Taft-Hartley Act in cases involving both unions and employers. It was established in the early 1960s that a union that engaged in discrimination among members of the bargaining unit on the basis of race violated its duty of fair representation, and engaged in unlawful restraint and coercion of employees under Section 8(b)(1)(A) of the Taft-Hartley Act. (Independent Metal Workers Union [Hughes Tool Co.], NLRB-1964, 56 LRRM 1289) Then in 1969, the U.S. Court of Appeals for the District of Columbia held that racial discrimination by an employer was unlawful interference under the Act. (Packing-

Issue	Holding	Comment
Civil Rights Act, Title VII: Substantive Rulings—Contd. Preemption: Taft-Hartley Act—Contd.		house Workers v. NLRB [Farmers Cooperative Compress], CA DC-1969, 70 LRRM 2489, 9 FEP Cases 317, rehear'g denied, 73 LRRM 2095, 9 FEP Cases 325, cert. denied, US SupCt-1969, 72 LRRM 2658, 9 FEP Cases 1407) But the NLRB later refused to accept the premise that employment discrimination based on race, color, religion, sex, or national origin was a per se violation of the Taft-Hartley Act as "inherently destructive" of employees' rights under the Taft-Hartley Act. It was a three-one-one decision, with Chairman Miller and Members Kennedy and Penello in the majority; Member Fanning concurred on the basis that there was insufficient evidence of discrimination; Member Jenkins dissented. (Jubilee Manufacturing Co., NLRB-1973, 82 LRRM 1482) Meanwhile, the U.S. Court of Appeals for the Eighth Circuit remanded a case to the NLRB for a determination on whether an employer could be ordered to bargain with a union that allegedly engaged in discrimination on the basis of race. (NLRB v. Mansion House Center Management Corp., CA 8-1973, 82 LRRM 2608, 9 FEP Cases 358)
	If a worker fails to obtain relief from the NLRB for allegedly being discharged in violation of the Taft-Hartley Act, he then may pursue a remedy for the discharge under Title VII. An adverse decision by the NLRB in a case brought before it, the U.S. Court of Appeals for the Sixth Circuit ruled, does not bar pursuit of a Title VII remedy. (Tipler v. E.I. du Pont de Nemours, CA 6-1971, 3 FEP Cases 540)	In so ruling, the court said that although the two laws are not totally dissimilar, their differences significantly overshadow their similarities. In the absence of a special consideration, a determination arising solely under one statute should not automatically be binding when a similar question arises under another statute.
Promotion Procedure: Firefighters	The entire procedure for the selection of firefighter lieutenants must be considered in determining whether the procedure had an adverse impact on black applicants in violation of Title VII. Although 35.9 percent of the white applicants passed a written test, the Fourth Circuit pointed out, the promotion procedure as a	The appeals court also upheld the lower court's findings that the city did not discriminate in discipline for chargeable accidents and in making fitness ratings. In a case decided three years earlier, the Sixth Circuit upheld a lower court's finding that a city's use of the Army General Classification Test as part of

Issue	Holding	Comment
Civil Rights Act, Title VII: Substantive Rulings—Contd. Promotion Procedure: Firefighters—Contd.	whole did not have an adverse impact on blacks, since 4.3 percent of the black applicants and 5.3 percent of the white applicants were promoted. One judge did not disagree with this conclusion, but objected to the court's affirmance of the lower court's conclusion that the black firemen were not entitled to relief, despite their claim of racial harassment. (Friend v. Leidinger, CA 4-1978, 18 FEP Cases 1052)	the process of hiring police officers did not discriminate against women. It noted that (1) of the only two women who had taken this test in applying for positions with the police department, one fared better than the national norm and the other lower, and (2) while testing and psychological data perhaps may forecast that women do less well on the test than men, these data are far from being "uncontroverted testimony" that women will fare less well. (Smith v. Troyan, CA 6-1975, 10 FEP Cases 1380)
	A city that used a firefighter promotional examination that had an adverse impact on black applicants and that was not job-related was ordered by the Eighth Circuit to promote 12 black applicants who passed the examination. The city had delayed in developing a nondiscriminatory method of selecting fire captains, the curt said, and this meant that it was continuing its policy of discrimination against black candidates who had been the victims of discrimination in the past. (Firefighters Institute v. City of St. Louis, CA 8-1978, 18 FEP Cases 1083)	In ordering the promotions, the court cited Regents of the University of Calif. v. Bakke, US SupCt-1978, 17 FEP Cases 1000, in which the Supreme Court "approved of the use of racial preference as a means of remedying constitutional or statutory violations resulting in identified race-based injuries to individuals entitled to the preference."
Promotions: Trainee under Affirmative Action	The failure of an employer to promote a black employee following his participation in an affirmative action training program does not prove racial discrimination under Title VII. Title VII cannot be interpreted to require that an employer guarantee a promotion to each and every black employee who participates, the Fourth Circuit ruled. To hold otherwise, "would impose so high a risk upon employers that their impulse to undertake any but the most innocuous and limited affirmative action efforts would inevitably be chilled." A lowering of standards designed to ensure that such a program works for each minority participant "can be expected to chill the zeal of employers voluntarily to undertake truly significant efforts." The holding is by a five-to-two margin, with the full court participating. (Wright v. National Archives and Records Service, CA 4-1979, 21 FEP Cases 4)	The dissenting judges asserted that the training program was "simply a pro forma exercise for nominal compliance with the requirements of an executive order and EEOC regulations without the attribute of equality that is essential to such a project." They also contended that the plaintiff had received virtually no training opportunities during the first six months of the two-year program and that substantially greater training was given to a white classmate.
Religious Discrimination: Accommodation—Saturday Sabbath	An employer made reasonable attempts to accommodate to the religious needs of an employee who, as a member of the Worldwide Church of God, refused to work on Saturday	This was the third time the issue had been brought before the Supreme Court. In 1971, the Court affirmed by an equally divided

Issue	Holding	Comment
Civil Rights Act, Title VII: Substantive Rulings—Contd. Religious Discrimination: Accommodation—Saturday Sabbath—Contd.	shifts, where the employer held several meetings with the employee to try to solve the problem, accommodated to his observance of special religious holidays, authorized the union to search for someone who would exchange shifts with the employee, and tried to find the employee another job. In reaching this conclusion, the Supreme Court made these other rulings: ● The EEOC's guideline construing Title VII's original ban on religious discrimination as requiring an employer to make a "reasonable accommodation" to the religious practices of an employee in absence of "undue hardship" is entitled to some deference, since Congress satisfied this guideline when it amended Title VII in 1973. ● An employer's duty under Title VII to accommodate to the religious practices of employees does not require it to take steps inconsistent with an otherwise valid collective bargaining contract or to deny shift and job preferences of other workers. ● Requiring an employer to bear more than a de minimis cost in order to give an employee Saturdays off because of his religious practices is an "undue hardship" within the meaning of Title VII. Requiring an employer to bear additional costs to give an employee Saturdays off when no such costs are incurred to give other employees a day off would involve unequal treatment on the basis of religion. ● Title VII's ban on religious discrimination will not be construed, in absence of clear statutory language or legislative history to the contrary, to require an employer to discriminate against some employees or to permit others to observe their sabbath. The decision was by a seven-to-two margin, with Justices Brennan and Marshall dissenting. (Trans World Airlines v. Hardison, US SupCt-1977, 14 FEP Cases 1697)	Court a decision by the Sixth Circuit that a company did not violate Title VII by discharging an employee who refused because of his religion to work on Sunday or to arrange for a replacement as required by the collective bargaining contract. (Dewey v. Reynolds Metals Co., US SupCt-1971, 3 FEP Cases 508) Then in 1976, the Court, again by an equally divided Court, affirmed another decision by the Sixth Circuit that an employer violated the provision of the 1972 definition of religion requiring an employer to make a "reasonable accommodation" to the religious practices of an employee when it discharged a supervisor who refused to work on Saturdays for religious reasons. (Parker Seal Co. v. Cummins, US SupCt-1976, 13 FEP Cases 1178) Because of the lack of a majority in these two cases, the holdings were not binding precedents.
Religious Discrimination: Union Security	An employer and a union made a sufficient accommodation to a worker's religious protest of a union security provision when they permitted him to substitute payment to a charity, including his own church, in lieu of paying union dues. The alternative accommodations proposed by the employee, which included	The employee also contended that it was against his religion to be compelled to make charitable contributions. But the court pointed out that the employee was not compelled to work for the company. It also pointed out that under the standards laid down by the Supreme Court in Trans World Airlines v. Hardison,

Issue	Holding	Comment
Civil Rights Act, Title VII: Substantive Rulings—Contd. Religious Discrimination: Union Security—Contd.	offering him a job outside the bargaining unit or exempting him from the union-security clause, are unreasonable, the Ninth Circuit concluded. (Yott v. North American Rockwell Corp. and United Auto Workers, CA 9-1979, 20 FEP Cases 870)	supra, the alternatives proposed by the employee were unreasonable, since they would be both costly and difficult to achieve.
Retaliation: General Scope of Protection	The protection against retaliation under Section 704(a) of Title VII does not give an employee unlimited license to complain of alleged discrimination. Upholding a lower court finding that the employee's discharge did not violate Title VII, the First Circuit explained that a balance must be reached between the purpose of protecting persons engaging reasonably in opposing discrimination and Congress' equally manifest desire not to tie the hands of employers in objective selection and control of personnel. On this basis, the appeals court upheld a lower court finding that a low "academic" evaluation given to a female scientist who had complained about alleged discrimination by a research institution was not retaliatory. The low evaluation triggered her discharge. (Hochstadt v. Worcester Foundation for Experimental Biology, CA 1-1976, 13 FEP Cases 804)	Like some of the other major federal labor laws, including the Taft-Hartley and Fair Labor Standards Acts, Title VII contains a prohibition against retaliation. Section 704(a) makes it an unlawful employment practice to discriminate against any employee, union member, or applicant for employment or union membership because he has opposed an unlawful employment practice or has filed a charge, testified, assisted, or participated in any manner in an investigation, proceeding, or hearing under Title VII. The prohibition applies to employers, employment agencies, labor unions, and joint labor-management committees controlling apprenticeship or other training or retraining programs.
	The decision in the Hochstadt case contrasts with an earlier one by the Fifth Circuit that a person filing charges of discrimination against his employer is protected against retaliation even if the charges are false or malicious. (Pettway v. American Cast Iron Pipe Co., CA 5-1969, 1 FEP Cases 752)	
	An employer engaged in unlawful retaliation by refusing to process an employment application until the applicant who had filed a charge with the EEOC against another company, settled his dispute with that company. (Barela v. United Nuclear Corp., CA 10-1972, 4 FEP Cases 831)	Although the employer contended that it rejected the applicant because it desired only permanent employees, the court ruled that the company failed to establish a business necessity defense.
Retaliation: Isolated Incident	The discharge of a white woman did not violate Title VII, even if her discharge was in retaliation for her opposition to a "racial slur" made by a male employee against a black woman employee in a conversation with the white woman. The Act is aimed specifically at eradicating discrimination by employers against em-	The court also rejected a contention that the employee was retaliated against by the employer because of her use of EEOC procedures. It pointed out that the employee neither contacted the EEOC nor threatened to do so until three days after she was fired.

Issue	Holding	Comment
Civil Rights Act, Title VII: Substantive Rulings—Contd. Retaliation: Isolated Incident—Contd.	ployees, the Ninth Circuit said. An extension of the ban against retaliation to "an isolated incident between co-workers," the court added, would clearly exceed the intent of Congress and the plain language of the statute. (Silver v. KCA, Inc., CA 9-1978, 18 FEP Cases 1199)	
Retaliation: Reasonable Belief of Discrimination	A Federal district court properly held that a city agency violated the Title VII ban on retaliation when it discharged a Mexican-American employee for writing a letter to the regional administrator of a U.S. Government agency complaining about hiring practices and job conditions, even though the court made no finding that the city agency actually was discriminating. The employee's opposition to the city agency's practices was based on a reasonable belief that they violated Title VII. The appeals court held, however, that the district court erred in ruling that because the unlawfully discharged employee failed to request reinstatement in his complaint, it was barred from considering such relief. Title VII gives a court discretion to order reinstatement of a wrongfully discharged employee. (Sias v. City Demonstration Agency, CA 9-1978, 18 FEP Cases 981)	The appeals court, however, remanded the case to the district court in view of its failure to make proper findings as to whether suitable alternative employment was available for the unlawfully discharged employee to support the finding that his efforts to mitigate damages were minimal.
Retaliation: Temporary Injunction	The 1972 amendments to Title VII gave the EEOC the right to seek temporary injunctive relief on behalf of an individual who files a charge under Title VII. In a case of first impression, the U.S. Court of Appeals for the Fifth Circuit held that an employee who alleged she was discharged because she had filed a charge with the EEOC had a right to bring her own action in a federal district court for temporary relief. (Drew v. Liberty Mutual Insurance Co., CA 5-1973, 5 FEP Cases 1077, cert. denied by US SupCt-1974, 8 FEP Cases 95)	The court reasoned that the employee should be granted relief to maintain the status quo pending the EEOC's investigation of her charge. It added that she established irreparable injury and the likelihood of ultimate success.
Reverse Discrimination: Consent Decree—Quotas	Section 706(g) of the Civil Rights Act of 1964 does not prohibit quota remedies. So a federal district court did not abuse its discretion when, over the objections of three unions, it (1) refused to modify a consent decree covering some 700,000 employees of the American Telephone and Telegraph Company and its subsidiaries providing for goals, intermediate targets, and "affirmative action override" in promotions, and (2) entered a supplemental order	The Supreme Court later denied review of the decision upholding the consent decree, despite the unions' contention that the seniority "override" provisions abrogated seniority rights under their collective bargaining agreements. (Communication Workers v. EEOC; Alliance of Independent Telephone Unions v. EEOC; US SupCt-1978, 17 FEP Cases 1095) Although the Supreme Court never states a reason for denying review of a case, some viewed the

Issue	Holding	Comment
Civil Rights Act, Title VII: Substantive Rulings—Contd. Reverse Discrimination: Consent Decree—Quotas—Contd.	intended to remedy the company's deficiencies in complying with the consent decree where, among other things, the court struck an appropriate balance between the integrity of the collective bargaining process and the necessity for effective relief under the Act, and the affirmative action override was applied only when necessary to bring particular work units into compliance. The U.S. Government has a sufficiently great interest in remedying the effects of a particular pattern of employment discrimination on the balance of sex and racial groups that otherwise would have justified, without violating the equal protection guarantee in Due Process Clause of the Fifth Amendment to the Constitution, a federal district court's entry of a consent decree providing for goals, intermediate targets, and an affirmative action override in making promotions. Such a decree would be lawful, even though the remedy could operate to the disadvantage of members of groups previously subject to discrimination who have not themselves been subject to discrimination. (EEOC v. AT&T Co., CA 3-1977, 14 FEP Cases 1210)	denial as evidence of a tolerance by the Court toward preferential treatment for minority groups that had not themselves been discriminated against. A second settlement of national significance was reached in 1974 between the government, the EEOC, and the Justice Department and nine major steel companies and the United Steelworkers' Union. In addition to providing back pay for 40,000 employees, the agreement set goals and timetables for filling openings in trade and craft jobs with women and minority-group employees. The settlement was upheld by the Fifth Circuit. (U.S. v. Allegheny Ludlum Industries, CA 5-1975, 11 FEP Cases 167)
Reverse Discrimination: Disparate Treatment	White employees who alleged that they were discharged by their employer for participating in misappropriation of cargo and that an employee who participated in this activity was retained, have stated a claim against the employer under Title VII. It is immaterial that the white employees' discharge was based on serious misconduct or crime. Title VII prohibits all racial discrimination in employment, and while crime may be a legitimate basis for discharge, it may not be the basis for racial discrimination. Title VII's terms, which are not limited to discrimination against members of any particular race, prohibits discrimination against white employees upon the same standards as it prohibits discrimination against black employees. The case was remanded by a unanimous Supreme Court, with Justice Marshall writing the opinion. But Justices White and Rehnquist dissented to Part III of the opinion because they did not agree that Section 1981 of the U.S. Code (1866 Civil Rights Act) does not extend protection to white persons. (McDonald v. Santa Fe Trail Transportation Co., US SupCt-1976, 12 FEP Cases 1577)	This decision was handed down three years before the Weber case, infra, was decided. In the majority opinion in Weber, Justice Brennan stated that the issue in Weber was expressly left open in the McDonald case. Weber argued that since the McDonald decision settled that Title VII forbids discrimination against whites as well as blacks, and since the Kaiser-Steel workers affirmative action plan operated to discriminate against white employees solely because they were white, it followed that the plan violated Title VII. Justice Brennan conceded that the argument was not without force. But it overlooked the significance of the fact that the Kaiser-Steelworkers plan was an affirmative action plan voluntarily adopted by private parties to eliminate traditional patterns of racial discrimination. In this context, Brennan concluded, Weber's reliance on McDonald was misplaced. In the dissenting opinion by Justice Rehnquist it was stated that the Court had never waivered in its understanding that Title VII "prohibits all racial discrimination in employment, without exception for any partic-

Issue	Holding	Comment
Civil Rights Act, Title VII: Substantive Rulings—Contd.		ular employees." He cited the McDonald decision, among others.
Reverse Discrimination: Education—Title VI	The Medical School of the University of California at Davis violated Title VI of the Civil Rights Act of 1964 by maintaining a special admissions program that totally excluded non-minority group applicants from 16 percent of the seats in an entering class. Title VI forbids racial discrimination in any program or activity receiving federal financial assistance. But the Court went on to hold that the school may establish an admissions program involving "competitive consideration" of race and ethnic origin. The holding was by a five-to-four margin, and there was no majority opinion. Justice Powell wrote the "principal" opinion in which he took the position that the school's action violated both Title VI and the Equal Protection of the Law's Provision of the Fourteenth Amendment to the Constitution. Four Justices wrote a concurring opinion, taking the position that the school violated Title VI and that it was not necessary to reach the constitutional issue. The four dissenting Justices took the position that there was no violation of either Title VI or the Constitution. (Regents of the University of California v. Bakke, US SupCt-1978, 17 FEP Cases 1000)	Although the decision in Bakke was in an educational rather than employment context, there was language in the opinions suggesting that it could be translated to the employment area, and many attorneys in the field so construed it. There were 52 briefs filed by over 200 attorneys in the case, attesting to the importance with which it was regarded. In Steelworkers v. Weber (Kaiser Aluminum Co.), discussed below, the Supreme Court decided a case directly related to employment.
Reverse Discrimination: Quotas—Training Programs	Title VII does not forbid *private* employers and unions from voluntarily agreeing upon bona fide affirmative action plans that accord racial preferences in the manner and for the purpose provided in the on-the-job training programs set up under an affirmative action plan voluntarily adopted by Kaiser Aluminum Company and the Steelworkers Union. The plan imposed a one-to-one ratio for whites and blacks for admission to the training program. When a white employee was denied admission to the program under the one-to-one ratio, while blacks with less seniority were admitted, he filed an action under Title VII. Both the district court and the Fifth Circuit ruled in favor of the white employee, Brian Weber. (Weber v. Kaiser Alum. & Chemical Corp., USDC ELa-1976, 12 FEP Cases 1615, CA 5-1977, 16 FEP Cases 1) The case was carried to the Supreme Court, with Weber on one side and Kaiser and the Steelworkers on the other. The decisions below	The majority opinion stressed the narrowness of the issue it was deciding. It made these points: ● Since the Kaiser-Steelworkers plan did not involve state action, the case did not present an alleged violation of the Equal Protection Clause of the Constitution. ● Further, since the plan was adopted voluntarily, the Court was not concerned with what Title VII requires or what a court may do to remedy a past proven violation of the Act. ● So the only question before the Court was the narrow statutory issue whether Title VII *forbids* private employers and unions from voluntarily agreeing upon bona fide affirmative action plans that accord racial preference in the manner and for the purpose provided in the Kaiser-Steelworkers plan. ● In this context, reliance on a literal interpretation of Sections 703(a) and (d) is misplaced. Those sections make it unlawful to

Issue	Holding	Comment
Civil Rights Act, Title VII: Substantive Rulings—Contd. Reverse Discrimination: Quotas—Training Programs—Contd.	were reversed by a vote of five to two, with Justices Stevens and Powell not participating. Justice Brennan wrote the majority opinion, joined in by Justices Stewart, White, Marshall, and Blackmun. Chief Justice Burger and Justice Rehnquist dissented. (Steelworkers v. Weber Kaiser Alum. & Chemical Co., US SupCt-1979, 20 FEP Cases 1)	discriminate because of race in hiring and in the selection of apprentices for training programs. Justice Blackmun wrote a concurring opinion in which he emphasized that, while the Court's opinion does not foreclose other forms of affirmative action, the program it approved is a moderate one. It does not afford an absolute preference for blacks, and it ends when the racial composition of Kaiser's craft work force matches the racial composition of the local population. By narrowing the holding and making clear that it was not considering certain issues the Court left significant questions unanswered. These include: ● What would be the status of an affirmative action plan for providing racial preference that is not voluntarily agreed to by the parties? ● What about the practices of the Office of Federal Contract Compliance Programs under which threats of debarment and actual debarment are used to require government contractors to adopt affirmative action programs? ● What if a plan is not "moderate," as Justice Blackmun describes the Kaiser-Steelworkers plan? Would it be upheld?
	NOTE: Prior to the decisions of the Supreme Court in the Weber, McDonald, and Bakke cases, appeals courts had handed down a number of rulings involving reverse discrimination, and the Supreme Court had denied review of two of them. The Eighth Circuit, for example, set aside a lower court order giving "absolute preference" to 20 minority-group applicants who meet revised qualification standards for the jobs. (Carter v. Gallagher, CA 8-1971, 3 FEP Cases 900, cert. denied, US SupCt-1972, 4 FEP Cases 771) But the Third Circuit upheld the Labor Department's "goals" for minority-group employment on federally financed construction, and the Supreme Court denied review. (Contractors Ass'n. of Eastern Pa. v. Hodgson, CA 3-1971, 3 FEP Cases 395, cert. denied by US SupCt-1971, 3 FEP Cases 1030)	
Reverse Discrimination: Quotas—U.S. Constitution	An affirmative action plan adopted by a police department that provides preferential treatment for black employees and applicants does not violate the rights of white persons under the Equal Protection Clause of the Fourteenth Amendment to the U.S. Constitution if (1) there	In addition to ruling on the constitutional questions, the court also held that the affirmative action plan did not violate Title VII. The validity of the plan under Title VII, it said, turns on whether it was effected to comply with the constitutional duty to remedy prior

Issue	Holding	Comment
Civil Rights Act, Title VII: Substantive Rulings—Contd. Reverse Discrimination: Quotas—U.S. Constitution—Contd.	is a sound basis for concluding that the minority group under representation is substantial and chronic and that the handicap of past discrimination is impeding their access and promotion, (2) no discrete group or individual is stigmatized, (3) the use of race is reasonable in the light of the objectives of the plan, and (4) no other approach offers a practical means of achieving the ends of the remedial program in the foreseeable future. In support of this holding, the court made the following additional rulings: ● Whether the 50-50 racial promotion provision of the plan is reasonable depends on the urgency of effectuating the objectives of the plan, the practical limitations in doing so, and the degree of hardship to be borne by whites. ● The city offered substantial justification for its police department affirmative action plan by its argument that a greater number of minority-group officers will result in improved law enforcement in that effective prevention and solution depend heavily on public support and cooperation, which results only from public respect and confidence in the police. ● A ratio requirement that is equivalent to the racial proportion of the labor market ordinarily achieves racial balance that would have existed but for discrimination. ● A presumption is required by logic and fairness that, where racial discrimination has been purposeful and pervasive, all racial imbalance within the discriminating organization occurred as its result. (Detroit Police Officers Ass'n v. Young, CA 6-1979, 20 FEP Cases 1728)	discrimination. On discriminatory intent, the court said that discriminatory intent, for the purpose of establishing liability under the Constitution, may be established by any evidence that logically supports an inference that the state action was characterized by an invidious purpose. In its ruling on the constitutional question, the court said that the opinion of Justices Brennan, White, Marshall, and Blackmun in Regents v. Bakke, supra, offered the most reasonable guidance.
Reverse Discrimination: Quotas—U.S., State Constitutions	A county civil service commission did not violate the Equal Protection Clause of the Fourteenth Amendment to the U.S. Constitution, Title VII of the Civil Rights Act of 1964, or the Equal Protection Clause of the California Constitution when it adopted a remedial race-conscious alternate-ratio hiring program, since the affirmative action program sought to eliminate established patterns of racial segregation and to open employment opportunities to minority groups from which they had been disproportionately excluded. The plan operated no more harshly on the rights of nonminority	The decision drew heavily on the opinions of the U.S. Supreme Court in both Steelworkers v. Weber, supra, and Regents v. Bakke, supra. It emphasized that the commission voluntarily was implementing affirmative action plans to overcome the continuing effects of past discrimination. In an earlier decision, however, a lower California court had invoked the California Supreme Court's Bakke decision in holding unconstitutional an order to integrate the City of Oakland's fire department by hiring and promotion quotas. (Hull v. Cason, Calif CtApp-1978, 18 FEP Cases 1379)

Issue	Holding	Comment
Civil Rights Act, Title VII: Substantive Rulings—Contd. Reverse Discrimination: Quotas—U.S., State Constitutions—Contd.	group persons than the plan approved by the U.S. Supreme Court in Steelworkers v. Weber, supra, and the plan is temporary in nature. The commission rule provided for imposition of the plan only after the commission found that the disproportionately low percentage of minority-group employees was caused by discriminatory employment practices, the "alternating ratio" orders sanctioned by the rule were specifically intended to ameliorate the effects of such identified discrimination, and the rule specifically provided that all orders issued pursuant to it would remain subject to continuing oversight so that they would not impose undue burdens on the needs of the department or on the interests of all interested parties. (Price v. Civil Service Commission of Sacramento County, Calif SupCt-1980, 21 FEP Cases 1512)	
Sex Discrimination: Benefit, Pension Plans	A requirement that women make contributions to a contributory retirement, disability, and death benefit program that were 14.8 percent higher than those required of men was unlawful discrimination based on sex under Title VII. The monthly benefits for men and women of the same age, seniority, and salary were equal. But based on a study of mortality tables and its own experience, the employer determined that women live longer than men. So it required the women to make higher contributions to the program. In holding the higher contributions required of the women a violation of Title VII, the Supreme Court observed that the basic policy of Title VII requires a focus on fairness to individuals, rather than on fairness to classes. A generalization that women as a class outlive men as a class cannot justify an extra assessment against female employees to whom it does not apply. The decision was by a seven-to-two margin, with Justice Stevens concurring in the judgment and concurring in part in the opinion. Chief Justice Burger and Justice Rehnquist concurred in part and dissented in part. (City of Los Angeles v. Manhart, US SupCt-1978, 17 FEP Cases 395)	The Los Angeles program later was amended so that there was no distinction, either in contributions or benefits, between the sexes. Prior to the Supreme Court's decision, there had been a disagreement between the EEOC and the Labor Department on such benefit and pension plans. In enforcing the Equal Pay Act, the Labor Department took the position that a plan would be lawful if it met one of these two tests: (1) The employer's contributions are equal for men and women performing equal work, or (2) the benefits under the plan are equal for men and women performing equal work. Under the EEOC's view, all aspects of an insurance, retirement, profit-sharing, or other fringe benefit plan had to be equal without regard to sex.
	A pension plan under which an employer makes equal contributions for men and women, but the male retirees receive larger monthly benefits than the female retirees violates the sex discrimination ban under Title VII. In so ruling, the	The First Circuit conceded that there could be very great difficulties in applying the Supreme Court's Manhart decision, supra, to an equal contribution—unequal benefits plan. A unisex plan would require additional funds, but the

Issue	Holding	Comment
Civil Rights Act, Title VII: Substantive Rulings—Contd. Sex Discrimination: Benefit, Pension Plans—Contd.	First Circuit rejected a contention that there was no discrimination because equal contributions were made for men and women. It pointed out that the contributions are not made in the form of a payment with which an employee may do whatever he or she desires. Instead, the contributions may be used only to buy an annuity or life insurance policy "with the foreknowledge that the woman's dollar can buy a different amount in those markets than can a man's." (EEOC v. Colby College, CA 1-1978, 18 FEP Cases 1125)	subsidy would be based on sex and would have to be at a variable rate, the court observed. It also pointed out that each female employee would end up with a pension contract that actually would be worth more than the one received by the male counterpart. If a plan permits surrender by the employee for a lump sum, the surrender value of the female employee's contract would exceed that of her male counterpart if fairly based on actuarial worth. One judge concurred in the decision, but expressed reservations on the court's commenting on the problems created by the Manhart opinion and its own decision.
Sex Discrimination: Clothing Requirements	An employer violated the sex discrimination provisions of Title VII by requiring female employees to wear uniforms, while giving male employees the freedom to wear normal business attire, even including leisure suits, so long as a suitable shirt and tie were worn. Title VII, the court pointed out, forbids an employer to discriminate on the basis of sex with respect to "compensation, terms, conditions, or privileges of employment." One judge dissented. He argued that the employer's policy did not limit the women in a way that tended to deprive them of employment opportunities. So there was no discrimination as to conditions of their employment. (Carroll v. Talman Federal S & L Ass'n, CA 7-1979, 20 FEP Cases 764)	In upholding the company's policy, the district court relied on a Ninth Circuit holding that there was no violation of Title VII in a retail chain's requirement that male employees wear a tie. (Fountain v. Safeway Stores, CA 9-1977, 15 FEP Cases 96) But the Seventh Circuit said that all the Ninth Circuit held in Safeway was that the employer may promulgate different personal appearance regulations for males and females.
Sex Discrimination: Congressional Employee	A woman who charged she was terminated by a Congressman because of her sex may be able to maintain a damage action against the Congressman, who is no longer in office, directly under the Fifth Amendment to the U.S. Constitution. The equal protection component of the Due Process Clause of the Amendment confers on the plaintiff a right to be free from gender discrimination that does not serve "important governmental objectives" and that is not "substantially related to the achievement of those objectives." The decision was by a five-to-four margin, with Chief Justice Burger and Justices Stewart, Powell, and Rehnquist dissenting. (Davis v. Passman, US SupCt-1979, 19 FEP Cases 1390)	In the majority opinion, the Court noted that while a lawsuit against a Congressman for putatively unconstitutional actions taken in the course of his official conduct does raise "special concerns counseling hesitation," these concerns are coextensive with the protections afforded by the Constitution's Speech or Debate Clause. If the ex-Congressman's actions were not shielded by that Clause, the Court said, he is as bound by the law as are ordinary persons. The case was remanded for a determination whether his conduct was protected by the Clause. The case later was settled.

Issue	Holding	Comment
Civil Rights Act, Title VII: Substantive Rulings—Contd. Sex Discrimination: Grooming Standards	An employer who refused to hire an applicant for the position of copy or layout artist allegedly and solely because of the length of his hair did not violate the Title VII prohibition against employment discrimination based on sex. A hiring policy that distinguishes between men and women on the basis of grooming policy or length of hair is related more closely to employer's choice of how to run its business than to equality of employment opportunity, since the distinction is based upon something other than immutable or protected characteristics. The plaintiff, the Fifth Circuit said, relied on a subtle form of discrimination characterized as "sex plus." He read "sex plus" to include sex plus any sexual stereo type and since short hair is stereotypically male, requiring it of all men would violate Title VII. The court rejected this argument. Hair length is not immutable, and in the situation of employer vis à vis employee enjoys no constitutional protection. If the employee objects to the grooming code, he has the right to reject it by looking elsewhere for employment or, alternatively, he may choose to subordinate his preference by accepting the code along with the job. The decision was by a 15-judge court. (Willingham v. Macon Telegraph Publishing Co., CA 5-1975, 9 FEP Cases 189) It reversed a decision by a panel of the court (5 FEP Cases 1329). Four judges dissented.	At least six other circuits have held the same way. The D.C. Circuit said that an employer may maintain reasonable good-grooming regulations because the image of the employer created by its employees dealing with the public on company assignments affects its relations with the public. (Fagan v. National Cash Register Co., CA DC-1973, 5 FEP Cases 1335; Dodge v. Giant Food, Inc., CA DC-1973, 6 FEP Cases 1066) The Ninth Circuit reasoned that Title VII refers to unfair employment practices directed against individuals as a class because of sex, and hair length standards are not directed against a class because of sex. (Baker v. Calif. Land Title Co., CA 9-1974, 8 FEP Cases 1313) Because the policies were reasonable and applied evenhandedly, the Eighth Circuit said, slight differences in appearance requirements for men and women had only a negligible effect on employment opportunities. (Knott v. Missouri Pacific Railroad Co., CA 8-1975, 11 FEP Cases 1231; see also: Longo v. Carlisle DeCoppet & Co., CA 2-1976, 12 FEP Cases 1668; Earwood v. Continental Southeastern Line, CA 4-1976, 14 FEP Cases 694; Barker v. Taft Broadcasting Co., CA 6-1977, 14 FEP Cases 697)
Sex Discrimination: Height, Weight Requirements	A federal district court correctly concluded that Alabama's statutory minimum height and weight requirements for the position of correctional counselor had a discriminatory impact on female applicants, even though the statistics presented to the court involved national percentages rather than percentages concerning the actual applicants for Alabama correctional counselor positions. In so ruling, the Supreme Court found that a contention that the minimum height and weight requirements (five feet two inches and 120 pounds) were job-related did not rebut a prima facie showing that these requirements had a discriminatory impact on women, where no evidence was produced correlating these requirements with the requisite amount of strength thought essential to good job performance. Justice Stewart wrote the Court's opinion. Chief Justice Burger and Justices Rehnquist and Blackmun concurred in the	The Court gave weight to the EEOC guideline stating its position that the bona fide occupational qualification exception should be interpreted narrowly. But the Court ruled that the federal district court erred when it ruled that being male was not a bona fide occupational qualification for the position of correctional counselor in Alabama's all-male maximum security prisons. It cited expert testimony that the use of women as guards in "contact" positions in such prisons under existing conditions—which include dormitory living conditions, understaffing, and lack of segregation of sex offenders—would pose a substantial security problem directly related to the sex of the guard.

Issue	Holding	Comment
Civil Rights Act, Title VII: Substantive Rulings—Contd.	judgment and concurred in part in the opinion. Justices Marshall and Brennan concurred in part and dissented in part. (Dothard v. Rawlinson, US SupCt-1977, 15 FEP Cases 10)	
Sex Discrimination: Maternity Leave—Arbitrary Cut-off Dates	The U.S. Supreme Court ruled that two school boards violated the Due Process Clause of the Fourteenth Amendment to the Constitution by maintaining and enforcing certain rules relating to maternity leave. In one case, the rule required a pregnant teacher to take maternity leave without pay five months before the expected birth of the child. In the other case, the rule required a teacher to take maternity leave without pay four months before the expected date of birth of the child. Arbitrary cut-off dates, which begin at different times in the school year for different teachers, have no rational relationship to a valid state interest of preserving continuity of instruction, the Court reasoned. Simply requiring a teacher to give substantial notice of her condition would serve school boards' objectives just as well while imposing far less burden upon constitutionally protected freedoms. Moreover, one school board violated the Due Process Clause by maintaining and enforcing a rule forbidding a teacher to return from maternity leave until the beginning of the next regular semester following the date when the child attains the age of three months. This was so even though portions of the rule requiring the teacher to present a doctor's certificate attesting to her health or to take a supplementary physical examination and to wait until the next semester following the birth of the child were considered valid. In the other case, the Court also upheld a rule requiring the teacher to submit a medical certificate and guaranteeing her return to work no later than the beginning of the next school year following the determination of eligibility. (Cleveland Board of Education v. LaFleur, US SupCt-1974, 6 FEP Cases 1253; Cohen v. Chesterfield County School Board, US SupCt-1974, 6 FEP Cases 1253)	The decision upheld a ruling by the U.S. Court of Appeals for the Sixth Circuit, which found that the mandatory requirement for taking maternity leave violated the Equal Protection of the Laws Clause of the Constitution. (LaFleur v. Cleveland Board of Education, CA 6-1972, 4 FEP Cases 1070) The Supreme Court reversed a decision by the U.S. Court of Appeals for the Fourth Circuit, which upheld a mandatory maternity leave requirement. Both cases were brought before the 1972 amendments to Title VII, which extended coverage to employees of state and local governments. (Cohen v. Chesterfield County School Board, CA 4-1973, 5 FEP Cases 341)
Sex Discrimination: Maternity Leave—Reinstatement in Same Job	An employer violated Title VII by its policy of denying employees returning from maternity leave guaranteed reinstatement to jobs held prior to the leave, while guaranteeing employees returning from disability leave reinstatement to	The court pointed out that the company otherwise treats all employees returning from leave of absence, including maternity leave, the same. In its opinion, the court discussed the applicability of both General Electric Co.

Issue	Holding	Comment
Civil Rights Act, Title VII: Substantive Rulings—Contd. Sex Discrimination: Maternity Leave—Reinstatement in Same Job—Contd.	job held prior to leave. This policy treats employees returning from maternity leave less favorably than employees returning from disability leave and thus impermissibly deprives female employees of employment opportunities because of their different role. (In re: Southwestern Bell Telephone Co. Maternity Litigation, CA 8-1979, 20 FEP Cases 691)	v. Gilbert, supra, and Nashville Gas Co. v. Satty, infra. It cited Nashville Gas in support of its holding.
Sex Discrimination: Mothers of Preschool Children	Women with preschool children must be hired on the same basis as men with such children under Title VII. But "the existence of such conflicting family obligations, if demonstrably more relevant to job performance for a woman than a man, could arguably be a basis for distinction under Section 703(e) of the Act." So reasoning, the Supreme Court set aside a decision of the Fifth Circuit, which upheld summary judgment for an employer who refused to hire such women and remanded the case for full development of the facts concerning the existence of a bona fide occupational qualification. Justice Marshall agreed with the remand, but disagreed with the Court's "indication" that a bona fide occupational qualification "could be established by a showing that some women, even the vast majority with preschool age children, have family responsibilities that interfere with job performance and that men usually do not have such responsibilities." (Phillips v. Martin Marietta Corp., US SupCt-1971, 3 FEP Cases 40)	The EEOC's regulations stated that the exception for "sex as a bona fide occupational qualification" should be interpreted narrowly. The listed a number of situations in which the exception would not apply.
Sex Discrimination: Newspaper Advertising: Help Wanted	In a landmark decision, the U.S. Supreme Court held that a newpaper's rights under the First Amendment were not infringed by an order of the Pittsburgh Human Relations Commission forbidding the carrying of help-wanted advertisements in sex-designated columns. (Pittsburgh Press Co. v. Commission, US SupCt-1973, 5 FEP Cases 1141)	The Court reasoned that the advertisements were "commercial speech" not protected by the First Amendment.
	In one leading case, it was held that a newspaper publishing male-female jobs is not an "employment agency" within the meaning of Title VII. So it is not a violation, in the court's view, to publish help-wanted ads expressing a preference as to sex. (Brush v. Newspaper Printing Co., CA 9-1972, 5 FEP Cases 20, cert. denied, US SupCt-1973, 5 FEP Cases 587)	But the EEOC has taken the position that job orders that designate sex expressly or by implication violate the law.

Issue	Holding	Comment
Civil Rights Act, Title VII: Substantive Rulings—Contd. Sex Discrimination, Newspaper Advertising: Situation Wanted	The free speech provisions of the First Amendment to the Constitution invalidate a provision of the Pennsylvania FEP statute that forbids a newspaper to publish situation-wanted advertisements that specify or express in any manner the race, color, religious creed, ancestry, age, sex, or national origin of the jobseeker placing the ad. Such prior restraint is not necessary to promote the state's legitimate interest in prohibiting discriminatory employment practices, the Pennsylvania Supreme Court said. The statute would restrict the expression of the advertiser rather than the unlawful activity. The prospective employee's use of prohibited employment criteria, such as age, sex, and race, in an advertisement, the court added, cannot reasonably be said to aid an employer that might be predisposed to use such criteria. One judge dissented. (Pa. Human Relations Comm. v. Pittsburgh Press Co., Pa SupCt-1979, 18 FEP Cases 1709)	In defending the statute, the Pennsylvania Commission argued that the case is controlled by the U.S. Supreme Court's decision in Pittsburgh Press Co. v. Pittsburgh Human Relations Comm., supra. In that case the U.S. Supreme Court decided that it was not a violation of the First Amendment for an FEP Agency to forbid a newspaper to publish sex-segregated help-wanted advertisements. But the Pennsylvania Court distinguished the two cases.
Sex Discrimination: Pregnancy as a Disability—Company Plan	An employer did not violate Title VII by excluding pregnancy disability from the coverage of its disability benefits plan, since this exclusion is not a pretext for discrimination against women, and there is no proof that the "package" of risks covered by the plan is, in fact, worth more to men than to women. Gender-based discrimination does not result simply because an employer's benefits plan is less than all inclusive. There were four opinions in the case. Justice Rehnquist wrote the majority opinion; Justice Stewart concurred; Justice Blackmun concurred in part; and Justice Brennan and Marshall dissented. (General Electric Co. v. Gilbert, US SupCt-1976, 13 FEP Cases 1657) NOTE: Less than a year after the decision was handed down, Congress amended Title VII to do the following: (1) require employers to treat "women affected by pregnancy, childbirth, or related medical conditions for the same all employment-related purposes, including receipt of benefits under fringe benefit programs, as other persons not so affected but similar in their ability or inability to work." A controversial provision permitted employers to refuse to cover abortion under any health plan, temporary disability plan, or sick-leave plan unless an abortion was necessary to save the mother's life or abortion coverage was part of a collective bargaining contract. The amend-	The action by Congress overturned not only the Aiello and General Electric doctrines, but it also put an end to a controversy that had raged in the courts for many years. The courts had divided on the issue.

Issue	Holding	Comment
Civil Rights Act, Title VII: Substantive Rulings—Contd.	ment overturned the Court's decision in Gilbert v. General Electric, *supra,* and Geduldig v. Aiello, infra.	
Sex Discrimination: Pregnancy as a Disability—State Law	In a case involving the California disability law, the Supreme Court upheld the exclusion of normal pregnancy and child birth from the coverage of the state disability insurance program. The Court found that the exclusion was not unconstitutional as invidious discrimination in violation of the Equal Protection Clause of the Fourteenth Amendment. California has legitimate cost-saving interests in its disability insurance program. It is not required to subordinate or compromise its legitimate interests solely to create a more comprehensive social insurance program than it already has. It was a six-to-three decision, with Justices Brennan, Douglas, and Marshall dissenting. (Geduldig v. Aiello, US SupCt-1974, 8 FEP Cases 97)	In Footnote 20, the Court observed that the California insurance program "does not exclude anyone from benefit eligibility because of gender, but merely removes one physical condition—pregnancy—from the list of compensable disabilities." It added that only women can become pregnant, but that "it does not follow that every legislative classification concerning pregnancy is a sex-based classification."
Sex Discrimination: Pregnancy—Loss of Seniority	An employer that denied accumulated seniority to a female employee upon her return from pregnancy leave violated Title VII. (1) Employer's policy denied the employee specific employment opportunities that she otherwise would have obtained, and even if she had been able to gain a permanent position with the employer, she would have been subject to the effects of her lower seniority level for the remainder of her tenure with the employer; (2) unlike the situation in General Electric Co. v. Gilbert, supra, the employer has not merely refused to women a benefit that men cannot receive, but has imposed upon women a substantial burden that men need not suffer; and (3) the employer adduced no proof of business necessity, and the policy easily might conflict with the employer's own economic and efficiency interests. Justice Rehnquist wrote the opinion of the Court; Justice Powell wrote a concurring opinion in which Justices Brennan and Marshall joined. They concurred in the result and in the opinion in part. Justice Stevens concurred in the judgment. (Nashville Gas Co. v. Satty, US SupCt-1977, 16 FEP Cases 136)	The Court also ruled on the issue presented in Gilbert v. General Electric Co., supra, holding that the employer's policy of not awarding sick-leave pay to pregnant employees does not violate Title VII if it is not a pretext for discrimination. The Court said the policy is legally indistinguishable from the disability insurance program upheld in the General Electric case.
Sex Discrimination: Pregnancy—Unemployment Compensation	A Utah statute that made pregnant women ineligible for unemployment compensation for a period beginning 12 weeks before the expected date of childbirth and ending six weeks after	In another case decided between Aiello and Gilbert, the Second Circuit held that the ruling in Aiello did not require the dismissal of an action under Title VII claiming that the

Issue	Holding	Comment
Civil Rights Act, Title VII: Substantive Rulings—Contd. Sex Discrimination: Pregnancy—Unemployment Compensation — Contd.	childbirth violates the Due Process Clause of the Constitution under the principles stated in LaFleur v. Cleveland Board of Education, supra. (Turner v. Department of Employment Security, US SupCt-1975, 11 FEP Cases 721)	company violated Title VII by excluding normal pregnancy from sickness and disability benefits under a collective bargaining contract. The court stressed that Aiello raised a constitutional issue involving due process and equal protection of the laws, while the case it was deciding involved statutory interpretation. So it found a violation of Title VII in the company's exclusion of normal pregnancy from disability benefits under a collective bargaining contract (Communication Workers v. A.T.& T. Co., CA 2-1975, 10 FEP Cases 435) The Supreme Court granted review of the case, vacated the judgment, and remanded the case to the Second Circuit for further consideration in the light of General Electric Co. v. Gilbert, supra. (A.T. & T. v. Communication Workers, US SupCt-1977, 14 FEP Cases 203)
Sex Discrimination: Veterans Preference	A Massachusetts veterans preference statute that has a disproportionate adverse effect upon women does not deny them equal protection of the law in violation of the Fourteenth Amendment to the Constitution where no intent to discriminate against women has been proved. The fact that the State Legislature, in enacting the veterans preference statute, made an intentional decision to grant preference to veterans and knew that most veterans were men does not warrant a conclusion that the legislature was motivated by an impermissible intent to discriminate against women. "Discriminatory purpose" implies more than intent as volition or as awareness of consequences; it implies that legislature was motivated at least in part "because of" not merely "in spite of" foreseeable adverse effects of the statute on women. There were three opinions: a majority opinion by Justice Stewart, a concurring opinion by Justice Stevens in which Justice White joined, and a dissenting opinion by Justice Marshall in which Justice Brennan joined. (Personnel Administrator of Mass. v. Feeney, US SupCt-1979, 19 FEP Cases 1377)	In the concurring opinion by Justices Stevens and White, it is noted that 1,867,000 men are disadvantaged by the challenge veterans preference. This number, it is asserted, is sufficient and sufficiently close to the number of disadvantaged women (2,954,000) to preclude a finding of an intent to discriminate against women. The dissenting justices contended that the choice of an absolute veterans preference evinces a purposeful gender-based discrimination.
Sexual Harassment: Advances by Supervisor	An employer would be liable under the doctrine of *respondeat superior* to a black female former employee who alleged she was discharged because she refused her supervisor's demand for sexual favors, even though what the supervisor	The courts had been divided on whether sexual harassment on the job is a violation of Title VII. But three other circuits have held in line with the Ninth Circuit that a female employee has a Title VII claim if her employ-

Issue	Holding	Comment
Civil Rights Act, Title VII: Substantive Rulings—Contd. Sexual Harassment: Advances by Supervisor—Contd.	was alleged to have done violated company policy. Title VII defines the types of wrongs for which an employer may be liable. A rule exonerating the employer for a tort committed by one of its employees acting in the course of his employment would create "an enormous loophole." (Miller v. Bank of America, CA 9-1979, 20 FEP Cases 462) The district court that rejected the charges said that if an isolated case of sexual harassment could succeed as a Title VII violation, there would be no end to allegations of sex-motivated considerations in cases of lost promotions, transfers, demotions, and dismissals. (Miller v. Bank of America, USDC NCalif-1976, 13 FEP Cases 439) Note: On March 11, 1980, the EEOC issued proposed guidelines on sexual harassment. (FEP Man. 401:185) They state: "Unwelcome sexual advances, requests for sexual favors, and other verbal or physical conduct of a sexual nature constitute sexual harassment when (1) submission to such conduct is made either explictly or implicitly a term or condition of an individual's employment, (2) submission to or rejection of such conduct by an individual is made the basis for employment decisions affecting such individual, or (3) such conduct has the purpose or effect of substantially interfering with an individual's work performance, or creating an intimidating, hostile, or offensive working environment." A woman who must endure sexual harassment in the workplace may gain relief under Title VII without having to show that she suffered a loss in benefits as a result of her refusal to submit to sexual advances of a supervisor. An environment of sexually oriented verbal or physical gestures is sufficient to violate the Act. As a remedy, the employer may be required to inform the employees that sexual harassment is illegal and to set up procedures for investigating and correcting sexual harassment. (Bundy v. Jackson, CA DC-1981, 24 FEP Cases 1155)	ment status is prejudiced because she rejected the sexual advances of her supervisor. (Barnes v. Costle, CA DC-1977, infra; Garber v. Saxon Business Products, CA 4-1977, 15 FEP Cases 344; Tomkins v. Public Service Electric & Gas Co., CA 3-1977, 16 FEP Cases 22) In the Garber case, the Fourth Circuit said that an employer commits a violation when it fails to take prompt and appropriate remedial action upon learning that a supervisor has made sexual advances toward a subordinate employee and has conditioned the employee's job status on a favorable response. In the Tomkins case, the Third Circuit said that Title VII is violated when (1) a supervisor, with actual or constructive knowledge of the employer, makes sexual advances toward or demands on a subordinate and conditions that employee's job status on a favorable response, and (2) the employer does not take prompt and appropriate remedial action after acquiring such knowledge. A district court said there could be sex discrimination not only where a male supervisor approaches a female subordinate, but also where a female supervisor makes demands on male workers. But the court added that there could be no finding of sex discrimination if the supervisor was bisexual and approached workers of both sexes equally. (Williams v. Saxbe, USDC DC-1976, 12 FEP Cases 1093) The D.C. Circuit, however, remanded the case for a trial de novo upon a finding that the trial court did not engage in either a true review of the administrative record or in an independent evaluation of the merits, but instead improperly accepted the nonfinal recommendation of a complaints examiner as the agency decision. (Williams v. Bell, CA DC-1978, 17 FEP Cases 1662) Upon remand from the D.C. Circuit, the district court reaffirmed its holding that the Community Relations Service of the Justice Department violated Title VII when it discharged a female employee who refused to submit to a male supervisor's sexual advances. (Williams v. Civiletti, USDC DC-1980, 22 FEP Cases 1311) Several district courts, on the other hand, have held that sexual harassment does not fall under Title VII at all. (See, for example, Corne v. Bausch & Lomb, Inc., USDC Ariz-1975, 10 FEP Cases 289, vacated and remanded on other grounds, CA 9-1977, 15 FEP Cases 1370)

Issue	Holding	Comment
Civil Rights Act, Title VII: Substantive Rulings—Contd. Sexual Harassment: Advances by Supervisor—Contd.	A female employee's asertion that her job at the U.S. Environmental Protection Agency was abolished because of her resistance to the sexual advances of her male supervisor stated a cause of action under Title VII, where it was contended that the supervisor did not make a similar approach to any male employee. Title VII outlaws conditions of employment for women that differ appreciably from those set for men and that are not genuinely and reasonably related to performance on the job. (Barnes v. Costle, CA DC-1977, 15 FEP Cases 345) A federal district court properly dismissed an action by a female professor who alleged that a college conditioned her continued employment on her acquiescence in alleged sexual advances by her department chairman. The court found that she had not alleged a sufficient nexus between her spurned advances and her termination, since she had not stated that the chairman had the authority either to terminate her employment or effectively to recommend her termination. (Fisher v. Flynn, CA 1-1979, 19 FEP Cases 932)	The court observed that an employer is generally chargeable with Title VII violations occasioned by discriminatory practices of supervisory personnel, although if the supervisor contravenes employer policy without the employer's knowledge and the consequences are rectified when discovered, the employer may be relieved from responsibility under Title VII. The court also observed that when Congress enacted the 1972 amendments to Title VII, extending coverage to the U.S. Government, it legislated for government employees essentially the same guarantees against sex discrimination that it previously had afforded private employees; therefore, anything constituting sex discrimination in private employment is equally interdicted in the U.S. Government sector.
Successorship Doctrine	Adopting a doctrine developed under the Taft-Hartley Act, the U.S. Court of Appeals for the Sixth Circuit held that a successor employer may be held liable under Title VII of the Equal Employment Opportunity Act to remedy unfair employment practices committed by the predecessor employer. The court stated that both statutes place emphasis upon extending protection to, and providing relief for, victims of prohibited practices. It added that Title VII was molded to a large extent on the pattern set by the Taft-Hartley Act. So decisions involving Taft-Hartley issues may be appropriate in resolving Title VII issues. In the Golden State Bottling case, the Supreme Court held that a successor employer who acquires its predecessor with knowledge that unfair-labor-practice charges had been filed against the predecessor and who continued the business without substantial interruption and change may be required under the Taft-Hartley Act to remedy its predecessor's violations. (Golden State Bottling Co., Inc. v. NLRB, US SupCt-1973, 84 LRRM 2839) The Sixth Circuit applied the same principle in the Title VII case. (EEOC v. MacMillan Bloedel Containers, Inc., CA 6-1974, 8 FEP Cases 897)	One thing stressed by the courts is that the successor employer must have notice of the charges so that it may take them into account in agreeing on a purchase price with the predecessor or an indemnity clause in the contract of sale.

Civil Rights Act of 1871

Issue	Holding	Comment
Civil Rights Act of 1871 Conspiracy Charge	A person whose claim of employment discrimination is cognizable under Title VII may not seek relief under the conspiracy portion of the Civil Rights Act of 1871. The conspiracy statute does not create any rights; it is a "purely remedial statute" that provides a cause of action when some otherwise defined federal right to equal protection is breached by a conspiracy. The conspiracy statute may not be invoked to redress violations of Title VII, since Title VII provides the exclusive remedy for employment discrimination. The decision was by a six-to-three margin, with Justices White, Brennan, and Marshall dissenting. (Great American Fed. S&L Ass'n v. Novotny, US SupCt-1979, 19 FEP Cases 1482)	The conspiracy provision of the 1871 Act authorizes a damage action for anyone who is deprived of the equal protection of the law or of equal privileges and immunities under the laws by a conspiracy of two or more persons. In this case, an employee who was a member of the board of directors of a savings and loan association supported complaints of sex discrimination that some of the company's female employees had lodged with the board. As a result, he alleged, he was not reelected to the board and was discharged. He sued under both Title VII and the conspiracy provision of the 1871 Act.
Ku Klux Klan Membership	A person who was discharged because of his membership in the Ku Klux Klan was denied relief by the U.S. Court of Appeals for the Fourth Circuit in a suit brought by him against his former employer and one of his supervisors. Although noting a Supreme Court decision that the 1871 statute applies to conspiracies by private persons, the appeals court stated that, under the circumstances, some state involvement has to be alleged by the Ku Klux Klan member to use the statute. The language of the statute follows that of the Fourteenth Amendment to the U.S. Constitution, the appeals court observed, and the Supreme Court has said that the section covers a wholly private conspiracy to deny black citizens the right to travel and rights based on the Thirteenth Amendment to the Constitution. But then it added that the language of equal protection chosen by the 1871 Congress may not be interpreted to mean that persons who conspire without involvement of government to deny another person the right of free association are liable under this statute. This is so, the court reasoned, because the right of association derives from the First Amendment, which was framed as a prohibition	The 1871 Act was one of a group of laws passed after the Civil War. They were not invoked in the area of employment discrimination until the 1970s. But they were invoked in cases in which charges of discrimination under Title VII had been dismissed. See above under "National Origin Discrimination: Citizenship" for a discussion of these cases.

Issue	Holding	Comment
Civil Rights Act of 1871—Contd. Ku Klux Klan Membership—Contd.	against the Federal Government and has never been extended to private persons. To make it so apply, the appeals court concluded, is an innovation that must come from Congress or the Supreme Court. (Bellamy v. Mason's Stores, Inc., CA 4-1974, 9 FEP Cases 1)	

Equal Pay Act of 1963

Issue	Holding	Comment
Equal Pay Act Constitutionality: Public Sector	Extension of the Equal Pay Act to states and their political subdivisions is a valid exercise of the power of Congress under the Commerce Clause of the Constitution; the Tenth Amendment does not bar the exercise of that power. In so holding, the Fifth Circuit distinguished the case from an earlier Supreme Court case in which the Court held that Congress lacked the power to extend the minimum wage and overtime provisions of the Fair Labor Standards Act (FLSA) to state and local government employees. The determination of minimum wages and maximum hours, the Court held, was reserved to the states and their subdivisions under the Tenth Amendment. (National League of Cities v. Usery, US SupCt-1976, 22 WH Cases 1064) Unlike the minimum wage and overtime provisions of the FLSA, the Fifth Circuit said, the Equal Pay Act does not displace a state's freedom to structure delivery of its services or employee relationships. "The Equal Pay Act leaves the states free to set all substantive terms of employment, provided that men and women receive equal compensation for equal work," the court said. It added that the ability to pay lower wages to female employees than to male employees for equal work is not one of the functions essential to a state's separate and independent existence. (Pearce v. Wichita County, CA 5-1979, 19 FEP Cases 339) A number of other courts have upheld the constitutionality of the Equal Pay Act on alternative grounds: (1) the Commerce Clause and (2) Section 5 of the Fourteenth Amendment. The Seventh Circuit upheld the constitutionality of the Act under the Commerce Clause. (Marshall v. City of Sheboygan, CA 7-1978, 17 FEP Cases 763) But the Third and Fourth Circuits relied on Section 5 of the Fourteenth Amendment alone in upholding constitutionality. (Usery v. Charleston County School District, CA 4-1977, 17 FEP Cases 597; Usery v. Allegheny County Institution District, CA 3-1976, 13 FEP Cases 1188, cert. denied US SupCt-1977, 14 FEP Cases 934)	Enacted in 1963 as an amendment to Section 6 of the Fair Labor Standards Act, the Equal Pay Act makes it unlawful for an employer to pay wages "at a rate less than the rate he pays employees of the opposite sex in such establishments for equal work on jobs the performance of which require equal skill, effort, and responsibility, and which are performed under similar working conditions." In 1976, the Supreme Court upheld the constitutionality of the 1972 amendments extending the coverage of Title VII to state and local governments. (Fitzpatrick v. Bitzer, US SupCt-1976, 12 FEP Cases 1586) This case is discussed above under "Civil Rights Act, Title VII: Substantive Rulings; Constitutionality: Public Sector."

Issue	Holding	Comment
Equal Pay Act—Contd. Equal Pay Standard	An employer violated the equal pay provisions of the FLSA by paying male night shift inspectors more than female day shift inspectors. The employer did not cure its statutory violation merely by permitting women to work as night shift inspectors nor by equalizing day and night inspector wage rates, but by establishing higher "red circle" rates for existing employees working on night shift. As used in equal pay provisions of the Act, the term "working conditions" encompasses physical surroundings and hazards but not the time of day worked. The decision was by a five-to-three margin, with Justice Stewart not participating. Chief Justice Burger and Justices Blackmun and Rehnquist dissented. (Corning Glass Works v. Brennan, US SupCt-1974, 9 FEP Cases 919)	In addition to ruling on the merits of the case, the Court also ruled on burden of proof. It held that the Secretary of Labor (now EEOC) has the burden of proving that the employer paid workers of one sex more than workers of the opposite sex for equal work. The burden then shifts to the employer to show that the differential is justified under one of the four statutory exceptions.
	Under the equal-pay standard, it is unlawful for an employer to pay wages "at a rate less than the rate at which he pays employees of the opposite sex in such establishments for equal work on jobs the performance of which requires equal skill, effort, and responsibility and which are performed under similar working conditions." In a leading case, the Third Circuit found a company in violation of the Act for basing wage differentials on an "artificially created job classification," which the court found appeared to have been intended to keep women in a subordinate role. (Shultz v. Wheaton Glass Co., CA 3-1970, 9 FEP Cases 502, amended 9 FEP Cases 508, cert. denied by US SupCt-1970, 9 FEP Cases 1408, on remand aff'd, vacated in part, and remanded 9 FEP Cases 647)	Skill, effort, responsibility, and working conditions are the tests of equality of work. But to be considered "substantially equal," in the view of the government, jobs are not required to be identical. There are exemptions for wage differentials paid pursuant to a seniority system, wage differentials paid pursuant to a merit system, and wage differentials paid pursuant to a system that measures earnings by quantity or quality of production.
Equal Work, Working Conditions Standard	In a case involving a differential between the pay of male orderlies and female aides in a hospital, the Sixth Circuit laid down these rules on equal work skills, effort, responsibility, and working conditions: ● A disproportionate frequency in the performance of the same routine tasks does not make jobs unequal under the Act. So any greater frequency with which male orderlies may have performed post-mortem work, as compared female aides, does not justify a wage differential favoring orderlies.	In hospital cases, the courts generally have found the work of female nursing aides and male orderlies to be "equal" under the Act, since the additional duties, responsibilities, or weight lifting was not substantial. But the Fifth Circuit has ruled that the issue of equality in these cases is a question of fact to be decided on a case-by-case basis. In one case, it affirmed a finding that the jobs were not equal (Hodgson v. Golden Isles Nursing Home, CA 5-1972, 9 FEP Cases 791) In another, however, it upheld a finding that the jobs were equal (Hodgson v. Brookhaven General Hospital, CA 5-1970, 9 FEP Cases 579)

Issue	Holding	Comment
Equal Pay Act—Contd. Equal Work, Working Conditions Standard—Contd.	● The application of the Act is not dependent upon job classifications or titles but rather depends upon actual job requirements and performance. ● Higher pay is not related to extra duties when the extra task consumes a minimal amount of time and is of peripheral importance. ● The burden of proving that a factor other than sex is the basis for a wage differential is a heavy one; the requirements for the exception are not met unless the factor of sex provides no part of the basis for the wage differential. Applying these rules, the Sixth Circuit reversed a lower court decision that had upheld the differential in favor of the male orderlies. (Brennan v. Owensboro-Daviess County Hospital, CA 6-1975, 11 FEP Cases 600)	
EPA's Relationship to Title VII: Affirmative Defenses	Female employees may maintain an action alleging that their employer deliberately paid them less than male employees for comparable work. The Bennett Amendment to Title VII, which states that sex-based wage differentials "authorized" by the Equal Pay Act are not unlawful under Title VII, incorporates into Title VII only the four exceptions to the Equal Pay Act and not its equal-work standard. (IUE v. Westinghouse Electric Corp., CA 3-1980, 23 FEP Cases 588)	In a case pending before the Supreme Court, the court will decide whether sex-based wage-discrimination claims asserted under Title VII are subject to a different standard of proof than the equal-pay-for-equal work standard applicable under the Equal Pay Act. (See Gunther v. Washington County, CA 9-1979, 20 FEP Cases 792; CA 9-1980, 22 FEP Cases 1650)
EPA's Relationship to Title VII: "Comparable Worth"	A city did not violate Title VII or the Equal Protection Clause of the Fourteenth Amendment by comparing its nurses with non city nurses for the purpose of determining their salaries, despite the contention that nurses historically have been underpaid because their work has not been properly recognized and almost universally has been performed by women, and, that therefore their salaries should be compared with those of nonnursing positions that they assert are of comparable worth to the city. The Bennett Amendment to Title VII generally is considered to have the equal pay-equal work concept apply under Title VII in the same way that it applies under the Equal Pay Act. (Lemons v. City & County of Denver, CA 10-1980, 22 FEP Cases 959) Note: The Third Circuit later handed down a contrary holding,	This was the first appellate case in which the EEOC's theory that Title VII requires equal pay for work of "comparable worth" was directly considered. The "comparable worth" standard was the subject of extensive hearings hold by the EEOC in 1980. In its opinion in the Lemons case, the Tenth Circuit cited an Eighth Circuit holding to the effect that: "We do not interpret Title VII as requiring an employer to ignore the market in setting wage rates for genuinely different work classifications." (Christensen v. State of Iowa, CA 8-1977, 16 FEP Cases 232) But see Fitzgerald v. Sirloin Stockade, CA 10-1980, 22 FEP Cases 262, in which the Tenth Circuit held that an employer violated Title VII in paying a female advertising manager a salary that did not reflect the responsibility she had in performing

Issue	Holding	Comment
Equal Pay Act—Contd. EPA's Relationship to Title VII: "Comparable Worth"—Contd.	stating that Title VII's ban against sex discrimination is not limited by the Equal Pay Act. (IUE v. Westinghouse Electric Corp. , CA 3-1980, 23 FEP Cases 588) The Lemons case was denied review by the Supreme Court, but a petition for review has been filed in the Westinghouse case.	a substantial part of the duties of a male advertising director.
Factors Other Than Sex	If a pay differential is based on a "factor other than sex" it is not unlawful under the Equal Pay Act. According to the Third Circuit, "factors other than sex" need not be job-related or typically used in setting wage scales. On this basis, the court upheld higher pay for salespersons selling men's clothes than that paid to those selling women's clothes. The distinction was based on a greater profitability to the employer. In holding such a differential permissible if based on legitimate business concerns, the court relied in part on the legislative history of the Act. (Hodgson v. Robert Hall Clothes, Inc., CA 3-1973, 11 FEP Cases 1271, cert. denied, US SupCt-1973, 11 FEP Cases 1310)	The "factor other than sex" exception to the equal-pay standard is in addition to the three specific exceptions for payments made pursuant to a seniority system, merit system, or a system measuring earnings by quality or quantity of production. In contrast to the Robert Hall holding, the Fifth Circuit held that a trial court did not apply an incorrect standard in determining that the jobs of clothes saleswomen and clothes salesmen and the jobs of seamstress and tailor in a department store require "equal skill, effort, and responsibility," within the meaning of the Act, even though the trial court used the term "similar" in comparing the jobs. (There was no instance in which this term was used to mean "comparable" rather than "a substantially equal.") A tighter market for salesmen and male tailors does not under the Act justify a department store's hiring men at a rate higher than that paid to obtain women with similar skills. (Brennan v. City Stores, Inc., CA 5-1973, 9 FEP Cases 846)

Executive Order 11246 (Government Contracts)

Issue	Holding	Comment
Executive Order 11246		
Affirmative Action: Federal, State Laws	In a case that arose in Ohio, the Ohio Supreme Court held that the low bidder on a contract for work on an Ohio college campus was properly denied the contract for failure to give unequivocal assurance of an affirmative action program for employment of blacks to conform with the requirements of Title VII, Executive Order 11246, and the Ohio Gubernatorial Executive Order. The said requirement is a reasonable requirement of the bid and does not constitute a guarantee of black employment so as to violate Title VII. (Weiner v. Cuyahoga Community College District, Ohio SupCt-1969, 2 FEP Cases 30) The U.S. Supreme Court later denied review of the case. (Weiner v. Cuyahoga Community College District, US SupCt-1970, 2 FEP Cases 337)	This is one of the rare cases in which both federal and state fair employment practice laws have been applied to a bidder on a government contract. The action was a taxpayer's action to enjoin the college from expending funds except to the lowest and best qualified bidder. One of the six justices dissented. For a district court decision upholding the Labor Department's revised Philadelphia Plan for minority-group employment on federally financed construction, see Contractors Ass'n of Eastern Pa. v. Schultz, USDC EPa-1970, 2 FEP Cases 472. The decision was upheld by the Third Circuit, and the Supreme Court denied review. (Contractors Ass'n of Eastern Pa. v. Hodgson, CA 3-1971, 3 FEP Cases 395; cert. denied by US SupCt-1971, 3 FEP Cases 1030)
Applicability: Absence of Contract	In two cases involving public utilities, the Fifth Circuit held that the utilities were subject to the Executive Order and regulations, even though they had never consented to be. (U.S. v. New Orleans Public Service, Inc., CA 5-1977, 14 FEP Cases 1734; U.S. v. Mississippi Power & Light Co., CA 5-1977, 14 FEP Cases 1730) Both decisions, however, were vacated and remanded by the Supreme Court for reconsideration in the light of the Court's decision in Marshall v. Barlow's, Inc., US SupCt-1978, 436 US 307. In the Barlow's case, the Court held that the Occupational Safety and Health Administration is not entirely exempt from the Fourth Amendment's prohibition of unreasonable searches and seizures in its conduct of warrantless administrative searches of commercial property. (U.S. v. New Orleans Public Service, Inc., vacated and remanded by US SupCt-1978, 17 FEP Cases 897)	In the New Orleans case, the company had raised a defense similar to that raised in the Barlow case, contending that the Executive Order and the regulations requiring employers to make records available for compliance review purposes constitutes an unreasonable search when applied to a contractor in the absence of contractual consent. One judge dissented, contending that the federal government may not impose a substantial contract obligation on a utility simply because the utility supplies energy to federal installations as required by state law and the terms of its state or municipal franchise. Upon remand, the Fifth Circuit decided that the case required further consideration in the district court. The district ruled that the U.S. was not violating the Constitution when it brought an action to require a government contractor to grant it access to the contractor's premises and records

Issue	Holding	Comment
Executive Order 11246—Contd. Applicability: Absence of Contract—Contd.		to determine whether the contractor was complying with Executive Order 11246, where the existence of an adversary hearing before the injunction was issued ensured that the standard of reasonableness mandated by the Fourth Amendment was met. (U.S. v. New Orleans Public Service, Inc., CA 5-1978, USDC La-1979, 21 FEP Cases 445)
Applicability: Government Leases	Does Executive Order 11246 cover government leases, and are regulations valid that specifically refer to leases? A federal court ruled affirmatively on both points. The court reasoned that the Executive Order is not limited to those circumstances in which the U.S. Government is the consumer of goods, services, or real property, rather than the supplier. (Crown Central Petroleum Corp. v. Kleppe, USDC Md-1976, 14 FEP Cases 49)	The case also involved an issue under the Freedom of Information Act (FOIA). The employer sought to prevent the Secretary of the Interior and the Director of the Office for Equal Employment Opportunity of the Interior Department from disclosing to a third person the Standard Form 100 filed with the Joint Reporting Committee under Title VII and Executive Order 11246. But the court said that neither Section 709(e) of Title VII nor 44 U.S.C. Sec. 3508 barred disclosure under FOIA of information obtained from a Government contractor pursuant to the Executive Order. The court found no merit to the contention that the information was supplied to the agency by the EEOC.
Applicability: Subcontractors	Workers compensation policies that an insurance company issues to government contractors are subcontracts under regulations issued pursuant to Executive Order 11246. However, Title VI and Title VII of Civil Rights Act of 1964 do not contain any express delegation of substantive lawmaking authority to the President and, therefore, may not justify application of Executive Order 11246 to insurance companies that provide blanket workers' compensation insurance to employers holding government contracts. (Liberty Mutual Insurance Co. v. Friedman, CA 4-1981, 24 FEP Cases 1168)	The court below held that the Executive Order was validly founded on the procurement statutes, Title VII and other sources, so that regulations issued pursuant to the Order, as applied to a government subcontractor are valid exercise of administrative authority. (Liberty Mutual Insurance Co. v. Friedman, USDC Md-1979, 21 FEP Cases 1016)
Debarment Procedures: Fair Hearing	Prior to hearings on the merits of which a government contractor is found guilty of noncompliance with Executive Order 11246, the U.S. Government may not take any action that disbars or has the effect of debarring the contractor from government contracts. So a federal district court properly invalidated regulations permitting a contractor to be debarred before hearing, the Seventh Circuit held, merely because one government agency had made a	The OFCCP's basic sanction for noncompliance with Executive Order 11246 is a formal contract debarment. But it also has used de facto debarment and contract passover policies. De facto debarment is achieved by simply not certifying to procurement officers that the contractor is responsible. Under the OFCCP's passover policy a contractor or bidder may be declared nonresponsible (but not more than twice) due to past noncompliance with the

Issue	Holding	Comment
Executive Order 11246—Contd. Debarment Procedures: Fair Hearing—Contd.	prima facie determination that the contractor had not complied with the Order. The court made the following additional rulings: ● A government contractor's appeal from a federal district court's decision upholding certain regulations that were issued pursuant to Executive Order 11246 is not moot, despite changes made in administration of the Order that appear to remedy some of the contractor's complaints about being passed over for contracts without a hearing. There still are circumstances in which contractors may be declared unawardable before a hearing. ● A regulation requiring a bidder on government contracts to certify that neither it nor any of its divisions, affiliates, or known first-tier subcontractors have received any written notification, such as a show-cause letter, alleging noncompliance with Executive Order 11246 is invalid as being inconsistent with the section of the Order requiring a hearing prior to debarment. The regulation debars recipients of show-cause letters from bidding on contracts, it prevents them from employing any first-tier subcontractors that have received show-cause letters, and it debars subcontractors from government contracts before a hearing, merely because of show-cause letters. ● The U.S. Government may publish the names of government contractors that are not complying with Executive Order 11246 only after hearings on the merits. ● Neither the regulation providing that a government contractor has not complied with Executive Order 11246 as long as it has an "affected class" problem nor the regulation requiring a government compliance agency to issue a show-cause letter after making a nonresponsibility finding to give the contractor an opportunity to avoid the enforcement procedure of the Order is inconsistent with the section of the Order requiring a hearing prior to debarment. A hearing on the merits is necessary to determine whether the contractor actually has an "affected class" problem, and the section requiring issuance of a show-cause letter does not debar a contractor from receiving contracts. (Illinois Toolworks v. Marshall, CA 7-1979, 20 FEP Cases 359)	EEO clause without receiving prior notice and an opportunity for a hearing. The debarment and passover policies have been successfully challenged in a number of cases in federal district courts. In directives dated September 8, 1978, and April 18, 1979, OFCCP modified its policies on debarment and passover to specify that it will not notify a contracting officer of determinations of noncompliance until the contractor has been afforded an opportunity for a hearing and will not ask contracting officers to delay award of a contract except as necessary to accomodate a hearing. There are exceptions where the contractor has not submitted, developed, or maintained an affirmative action plan, the plan lacks some vital element, or the contractor has harassed a compliance officer or has attempted to impede the review.

Issue	Holding	Comment
Executive Order 11246—Contd. Disclosure of Information: Affidavits of Charging Parties	In a case involving the disclosure of affidavits filed by employees and former employees in support of Title VII charges against an employer, the Fourth Circuit made these rulings: • The exemption under the Freedom of Information Act (FOIA) for matters specifically exempted from disclosure by statute does not apply to affidavits filed by charging parties with the EEOC in support of a charge against an employer, notwithstanding the provisions of Title VII forbidding the EEOC to make public charges filed with it and making it unlawful for an EEOC office or employee to make public, prior to the institution of any proceeding, any information obtained by the EEOC. • Affidavits of former employees were not exempt from disclosure under the exemption in the FOIA for investigatory records whose disclosure would interfere with enforcement proceedings. • Affidavits of present employees were exempt from disclosure under exemption in FOIA for investigatory records whose disclosure would interfere with enforcement proceedings. (Charlotte-Mecklenburg Hospital Authority v. Perry, CA 4-1978, 16 FEP Cases 680)	The Supreme Court has held that information submitted to the government by a government contractor pursuant to Executive Order 11246 is not exempt from disclosure under FOIA. For a discussion of this holding see below under "Executive Order 11246: Disclosure of Information." Also, the NLRB has held that a union bargaining agent that has a nondiscrimination clause in its contract is entitled to information concerning the employer's EEO practices. See above under "Taft-Hartley Act: Unfair Labor Practice Cases; Bargaining Obligations; Data for Bargaining-EEOC Information" for a discussion of the NLRB's holdings.
Disclosure of Information: Contractor's Data	A Government contractor that submitted information to the Defense Logistics Agency pursuant to Executive Order 11246 may not maintain an action under the Freedom of Information Act (FOIA) to prevent disclosure of this information to third parties, even though FOIA exempts specified items from mandatory disclosure. Congress did not limit an agency's discretion to disclose information when it enacted FOIA. Regulations of the Office of Federal Contract Compliance Programs (OFCCP) authorizing disclosure of information submitted by government contractors pursuant to Executive Order 11246 are not within the provision of the Trade Secrets Act that permits disclosure of confidential commercial information only if "authorized by law." Even though regulations were adopted pursuant to the section of the Order that directs the Secretary of Labor to adopt rules and issue orders necessary and appropriate to achieve purposes of the Order, regulations are not reasonably within contemplation of any arguable statutory grant of author-	The Court held, however, that the employer was entitled to a review under Section 10(a) of the Administrative Procedure Act (APA) of the agency's decision to disclose the information, since the Trades Secrets Act (TSA) places substantive limits on agency action, and any disclosure that violates the Trades Secrets Act is "not in accordance with law" within the meaning of the APA. Prior to the Supreme Court's decision in the Chrysler case, the circuit courts had divided on whether an agency may disclose privately submitted information even if an FOIA exemption is applicable. The Fifth, Eighth, and D.C. Circuits had held, along with the Third Circuit in the Chrysler case, that agencies had discretionary authority to make such disclosure. (See Pennzoil Co. v. Federal Power Commission, CA 5-1976, 534 F.2d 627; General Dynamics Corp. v. Marshall, CA 8-1978, 16 FEP Cases 898; Charles River Park "A" Inc. v. Department of HUD, CA DC-1977, 519 F.2d 941; Chrysler Corp. v. Schlesinger, CA 3-1977, 15 FEP Cases

Issue	Holding	Comment
Executive Order 11246—Contd.	ity for promulgation of the Order. The decision was unanimous. Justice Rehnquist wrote the opinion and Justice Marshall wrote a concurring opinion. (Chrysler Corp. v. Brown, US SupCt-1979, 19 FEP Cases 475)	1217) But the Fourth Circuit had held that the agencies do not have such authority. (Westinghouse Electric Corp. v. Schlesinger, CA 4-1976, 13 FEP Cases 868)
Sanctions: Back-Pay Remedy	Revised regulations issued by the OFCCP in 1977 asserted a long-claimed authority to require back pay as a remedy under the Executive Order. According to the OFCCP, the revision was intended only to clarify established policy. But the policy already has been the subject of litigation. In U.S. v. Duquesne Light Co., USDC WPa-1976, 13 FEP Cases 1608, the court refused to strike from an action brought by the government a provision seeking back pay for discrimination in violation of contractual and Executive Order covenants not to discriminate. In U.S. v. Lee Way Motor Freight, Inc., USDC WOkla-1977, 15 FEP Cases 1385, however, another court held that the Executive Order does not "provide for actions by the government for breach of contract to recover back pay." The court specifically refused to follow the earlier holding in the Duquesne Light case. The Tenth Circuit subsequently remanded the Lee Way case to the district court, with an order to consider whether the U.S. may seek back pay from a government contractor for the benefit of discriminatees under Executive Order 11246. (U.S. v. Lee Way Motor Freight, Inc., CA 10-1979, 20 FEP Cases 1345) The case later was settled.	Under current practices the OFCCP may investigate a contractor's past employment practices as part of a compliance review. It may determine that back pay is allegedly due and require payment before the contractor may be considered in compliance. Under this procedure, a contractor may be faced with a choice of agreeing to pay without a hearing or being considered not in compliance and "non-responsible" for a future award.
Sanctions: Debarment, Cancellation of Contracts	A government contractor that has been debarred from contracts for failure to comply with inspection and discovery procedures under Executive Order 11246 did not make a sufficient showing of irreparable injury to warrant issuance of an injunction pending appeal of a federal district court's decision upholding debarment, where the Secretary of Labor has assured the court that if it ultimately finds the discovery regulations invalid that the contractor is challenging, any information provided by the contractor to the government under these regulations will be excluded from the evidence and struck from the record of any subsequent administrative proceedings. (Uniroyal, Inc. v. Marshall, CA DC-1979, 20 FEP Cases 446)	The decision by the D.C. Circuit was the fifth in this bitterly litigated case. First, an administrative law judge issued a recommended decision canceling existing Uniroyal government contracts and debarring it from future contracts. Uniroyal filed 43 exceptions to the law judge's findings and recommended decision. But the Secretary of Labor rejected all the exceptions and adopted the recommended decision. (Uniroyal Inc., v. Marshall, Sec.Lab-1979, 20 FEP Cases 419) The Secretary of Labor's decision was upheld by the district court on a motion for summary judgment, although the debarment order was modified to give Uniroyal the right to be relieved from debarment upon compliance with the inspection and discovery regulations. (Uniroyal, Inc.,

Issue	Holding	Comment
Executive Order 11246—Contd. Sanctions: Debarment, Cancellation of Contracts—Contd.		v. Marshall, USDC DC-1979, 20 FEP Cases 437) Before this case was decided, a federal district court in Indiana had denied Uniroyal's complaint for declaratory and injunctive relief to enjoin the OFCCP in the Labor Department from holding a hearing on sanctions against Uniroyal. The court found that Uniroyal had failed to exhaust the administrative procedures. (Uniroyal, Inc. v. Marshall, USDC NInd-1977, 20 FEP Cases 417)
Sanctions: Debarment Procedures—Exhaustion of Remedies	A government contractor is required to exhaust administrative remedies before it may maintain a court challenge to regulations of the Office of Federal Contract Compliance Programs (OFCCP), despite the contractor's contention that it has raised important questions of law concerning statutory interpretations. A review of challenged regulations is particularly desirable where, as in this case, the challenge is to the regulations as applied to a specific set of facts, as well as to the regulations on their face. (CA 10-1979, 18 FEP Cases 1635) The Supreme Court denied review of the case. (St. Regis Paper Co. v. Marshall, US SupCt-1979, 20 FEP Cases 1473)	The company argued that agency review would be expensive and fruitless and that the agency rules constitute "final action" subject to pre-enforcement court review. But the court rejected these arguments as not entitling the company to avoid having to exhaust administrative remedies before it may maintain a court challenge to the regulation. It will not be assumed, the court observed, that the agency will deny the contractor relief to which it is entitled. Even if final agency action is at issue, the controversy is not "ripe" for court resolution where further and adequate administrative relief has been requested but not exhausted. The court also held that the contractor had not made a sufficient showing of irreparable injury to excuse it from the exhaustion of administrative remedies by showing (1) that it is subject to de facto debarment from government contracts due to outstanding show-cause notice at one facility and (2) it continues to be subject to show-cause notices at its other facilities.
Sanctions: "Nonresponsible" Designation	The OFCCP has taken the position that it may designate a company as "nonresponsible" for government contracts because of alleged deficiencies in its affirmative action program without a hearing. This designation "nonresponsible" means that the company does not have the capability to perform the contract and therefore is ineligible for its award. The OFCCP regulations, however, state that once a company has been passed over for more than one contract, the OFCCP is required to initiate enforcement proceedings. Moreover, the OFCCP apparently has represented its position to be that where two such passovers have occurred, a hearing is required prior to any additional passovers for the same deficiency. (See Crown Zellerbach	Similar restraining orders have been issued by other courts to bar the OFCCP from imposing sanctions without a hearing. (See e.g., Sundstrand Corp. v. Marshall, USDC NIll-1978, 17 FEP Cases 432; Illinois Tool Works v. Marshall, USDC NIll-1978, 17 FEP Cases 520)

Issue	Holding	Comment
Executive Order 11246—Contd. Sanctions: "Non-responsible" Designation—Contd.	Corp. v. Marshall, USDC ELa-1977, 15 FEP Cases 1628) The OFCCP has taken the position that "nonresponsibility" determinations are not de facto debarments or suspensions and fall within the permissible scope of administrative authority under the Executive Order. But some contractors have asserted that the practice imposes a penalty without a hearing and violates both the Executive Order and constitutional due process. The recent weight of authority in the courts appears to have accepted this assertion. In Pan American Airways v. Marshall, USDC SNY-1977, 15 FEP Cases 1607, the court issued a preliminary injunction barring the government from taking any adverse action against the contractor regarding its contracts without a hearing. See also St. Regis Paper Co. v. Usery, USDC Colo-1977, 14 FEP Cases 1641, in which the court held that no preliminary injunction was necessary following a show-cause notice, since the OFCCP had determined that the controversy involved "substantial issues of law or fact." But the court added that an injunction would have been issued if irreparable injury was about to occur. The decision later was affirmed by the Tenth Circuit, St. Regis Paper Co. v. Marshall, CA 10-1979, 18 FEP Cases 1635; and the Supreme Court denied review, US SupCt-1979, 20 FEP Cases 1473. For discussion of another aspect of this case, see above under "Debarment Procedures: Exhaustion of Remedies."	

Rehabilitation Act of 1973 (Handicapped Workers)

Issue	Holding	Comment
Rehabilitation Act of 1973 (Handicapped Workers) **Private Employer**	A former employee who alleged that a private nursing home terminated her because of impaired eyesight does not have a claim that falls within the scope of the Rehabilitation Act of 1973. The action was brought under Section 504 of the Act, which forbids discrimination against the handicapped by a recipient of federal financial assistance. But the court stated that there is no indication that Congress intended to provide a private right of action in such cases. Moreover, it added, the funds received by the home were not federal assistance but were payment for services rendered. (Trageser v. Libbie Rehabilitation Center, CA 4-1978, 18 FEP Cases 1141) The Fifth Circuit later ruled the same way, holding that Section 503 of the Rehabilitation Act may not be construed as creating a private right of action to remedy alleged handicapped worker discrimination by federal contractors. (Rogers v. Frito-Lay, Inc., CA 5-1980, 22 FEP Cases 16) See also Carmi v. Metropolitan St. Louis Sewer District, CA 8-1980, 22 FEP Cases 1107, in which an unsuccessful handicapped job applicant was held to lack standing to sue a sewer agency which received federal financial assistance in the form of construction and engineering grants for a treatment plant. The court said the applicant was not an intended beneficiary of federal assistance. The Seventh Circuit also held that Congress did not intend to create a private right of action to remedy violations of Section 503 of the Rehabilitation Act. In another ruling in the same case, however, the court held that a former employee who was suffering from alcoholism had standing as a "handicapped individual" under Section 504 of the Rehabilitation Act where his employer had failed to show that his alcoholism prevented his successful performance on the job. (Simpson v. Reynolds Metals Co., CA 7-1980, 23 FEP Cases 868)	The Rehabilitation Act of 1973 prohibits employment discrimination, but its scheme is very different from that of most employment discrimination statutes. Section 501 imposes a duty on U.S. Government agencies to take affirmative action to hire, place, and advance handicapped individuals. Section 503 forbids discrimination against the handicapped by employees holding government contracts. The district courts have divided on the question whether there is a private right of action under the Act. A private right of action was implied in Drennon v. Philadelphia General Hospital, USDC EPa-1977, 14 FEP Cases 1385; Duran v. City of Tampa, USDC MFla-1977, 17 FEP Cases 914; Hart v. County of Alameda, USDC NCalif-1979, 21 FEP Cases 233; and Chaplin v. Consolidated Edison Co., USDC SNY-1980, 21 FEP Cases 1417. But other district courts have held there is no private right of action under Section 503. (See Rogers v. Frito-Lay, Inc., USDC NTex-1977, 14 FEP Cases 1752 [upheld by CA 5]; Wood v. Diamond State Telephone Co., USDC Del-1977, 18 FEP Cases 647) The courts in the Drennan and Duran cases found a private right of action under Section 504, the section invoked in the Trageser cases, as well as under Section 503. Another court found a private right to sue in a class action brought against a city by former drug users enrolled in a methadone program. (Davis v. Bucher, USDC EPa-1978, 17 FEP Cases 918) A professor who alleged that a college discriminated against him because of his alcoholism was held entitled to maintain an action under Section 504 of the Act and was not required to exhaust administrative remedies before bringing the suit. (Whitaker v. Board of Higher Education, USDC ENY-1978, 18 FEP Cases 906)

Issue	Holding	Comment
Rehabilitation Act of 1973 (Handicapped Workers)—Contd. **U.S. Government Agency**	A U.S. Government agency is not "a program or activity receiving federal financial assistance" that may be sued for handicapped worker discrimination under Section 504 of the Rehabilitation Act. Government agencies are specifically covered by the affirmative action program requirements of Section 501(b) of the Act, and regulations adopted under Section 504 define "recipient" and "federal financial assistance" in terms that when rationally construed do not apply to U.S. Government agencies. (Coleman v. Darden, CA 10-1979, 19 FEP Cases 137)	In the specific case, the court held that the EEOC did not act arbitrarily or capriciously when it failed to offer a blind law clerk a position of research analyst where his inability to read, among other things, rendered him less qualified to perform that job than the person ultimately appointed. The court noted: (1) The EEOC considered him for the position on the basis of his application and performance evaluation and examined his strength and weaknesses along with those of other candidates; (2) the EEOC provided readers with specialized training and skills for visually handicapped persons in the positions of law clerk and staff attorney, and so this conclusion seems reasonable in the light of the duties of the position; and (3) the expense involved in providing a reader for the job of research analyst cannot be considered irrelevant.
Definitions: Terms in Act	In a case designed to test Labor Department interpretations of terms used in the Act, the U.S. District Court in Hawaii made these rulings: ● Coverage under the Act extended to a contract held by a contractor that had at least one federal contract worth more than $50,000 at all relevant times and that employed more than 50 employees where the contract is valued at more than $2,500 and the contractor never requested that it be exempted from the Act. ● The intent of Congress in amending the definition of a "handicapped individual" to include persons "regarded as having such an impairment" was to protect people who are denied employment because of an employer's perceptions, whether or not those perceptions are accurate. ● The term "impairment," as used in the Act, does not need to be defined by reference to the American Medical Association Guides to the Evaluation of Permanent Impairment, since Congress is not required to spell out every possible condition of abnormality that could constitute an impairment. Dictionary definition is a broad but an entirely logical way of viewing the meaning of the term.	The case involved an apprentice carpenter who was denied employment because of a back ailment. A hearing was held before an administrative law judge, who found the physical examination used for the job did not tend to screen out qualified handicapped individuals. He recommended that the complaint be dismissed in its entirety. The decision was reversed by the Assistant Secretary of Labor, who ordered the company to offer the individual a job and comply with certain other requirements or be debarred from all government contracts. The court action was filed to obtain a review of the Assistant Secretary's decision.

Issue	Holding	Comment
Rehabilitation Act of 1973 (Handicapped Workers)—Contd. **Definitions: Terms in Act—Contd.**	● Assistant Secretary of Labor defined term "substantially limited" in an overbroad manner when he determined that an individual is substantially limited if the "impairment is a current bar to the employment of one's choice with a federal contractor in a job which the individual is currently capable of performing," where this definition includes any individual who is capable of performing a particular job and is rejected for it because of a real or perceived mental impairment. Congress did not intend to cover an individual who was denied employment by employer at one of its locations because of an impairment, but who was offered the same position at other locations. ● The proper focus in a proceeding under the Rehabilitation Act must be on the individual job seeker and not solely on impairment or perceived impairment. ● The determination whether an impaired individual is substantially limited or substantially handicapped in his employment within the meaning of the Act depends on (1) the number of jobs from which he is disqualified, (2) the types of jobs from which he would be rejected (3) the geographical area to which he has reasonable access, and (4) the individual's job expectations and training. The court granted a partial summary judgment to the Labor Department. (E.E. Black, Ltd. v. Marshall, USDC Hawaii-1980, 23 FEP Cases 1253)	

Table of Cases Cited

D

E

F

G

H

O

P

R

S

T

U